In the silence following the frenzied activity of funeral arrangements and people dropping in, the sad fact begins to sink in: life will never be the same again. You are definitely alone. With a lot to learn. As one friend put it: It took me twenty years to learn to live with my husband; I wasn't going to unlearn overnight. Neither will you.

Mourning is a natural and necessary process. It shouldn't be rushed. For in grieving over the loss of another, what we are really doing is grieving over our loss of self, all the self that was invested in that person.

Grief is an illness with recognizable symptoms—headaches, stomach aches, perhaps even a rash. A dreadful apathy can overtake you, and a withdrawal from reality. You lose contact with reality; you lose your trust in life.

Bereavement is a terrible mental wound, but it does heal. It just takes time. That's a terrible cliché and not quite true. It isn't going to go away all by itself. You have to work at it.

THE SURVIVAL GUIDE FOR WIDOWS

Betty Jane Wylie

Formerly titled BEGINNINGS: A Book for Widows

BALLANTINE BOOKS • NEW YORK

Copyright © 1977 by Betty Jane Wylie
Revised edition 1982

Originally published under the title
BEGINNINGS: A Book for Widows

The author and publisher gratefully acknowledge the
assistance of The Canadian Life and Health
Insurance Association in making this book possible.

ISBN 0-345-33008-0

Manufactured in the United States of America

First Ballantine Books/Epiphany Edition: July 1984
Second Printing: January 1986

Contents

Acknowledgments

This is a book that had to be written. It takes time to learn to be a wife. Perhaps it takes equal time to learn to be a widow, longer, because there's no one to help you learn. It is a more painful process and it is singular. Because I am by nature a communicative person I couldn't help expressing my feelings publicly about this process. I'd like to thank all the widows and widowers who have responded to me and whose comments I have quoted in these pages.

This is the book I wish I'd had when my husband died. I searched desperately for something to read, some bedside companion I could turn to every night that would assure me I wasn't going insane. This book has turned out to be that companion for other widows. If my pain has served a purpose, then it has been useful pain.

I'd like to thank David Shayne who helped me translate the technical parts of the book to the American market. A probate lawyer, with a great sympathy for and understanding of the needs of widows, he phoned me several years ago when he first read the book, foreseeing a time when it would become available to American readers. He offered to help me when that time came. I am grateful for his prophecy come true as well as for his generosity.

for Bill

1
The end and the beginning

It isn't for the moment you are struck that you need courage, but for the long uphill climb back to sanity and faith and security.

ANNE MORROW LINDBERGH

"Every beginning is hard," states a German proverb, and this is no exception. To begin a book with an ending is no way to begin, but this is where you and I come in.

There is no faster way to stop a conversation than to give a straight answer to someone you have just met who asks you, "Where is your husband?" At the moment of truth, the questioner indicates that he wishes the floor would open up and swallow him, and both of you are left at a loss for words. But you might as well get on with it.

Here goes.

My husband was a healthy, vigorous man who took good care of himself. We both worked out three or four times a week at a health club; we watched our weight—he more successfully than I—and we had yearly check-ups. At his most recent check-up Bill had been pronounced in excellent condition, cholesterol count low, recovery time good. He was forty-five years old, six foot three, and weighed 175 pounds. On our regular walks we were beginning to look forward to an active old age together. In short, if he were alive today, he'd be a very healthy man.

He burped shortly after Easter Sunday dinner in April, 1973, and died. Death by asphyxiation: the valve in his epiglottis failed to close again after the slight regurgitation, and food got into his windpipe, thence into his lungs and suffocated him within about eight minutes. He didn't know what hit him. Neither did we.

It is not as freaky a death as it might seem; there are statistics on it, and magazine articles are beginning to tell how to prevent such a death. Apparently it is more preventable if food lodges in the windpipe going down than if it sticks there on its way back up. That is merely academic. The fact is that Bill Wylie is dead.

We were having a nice life. We had been married for twenty years, had four children: two girls, Liz and Kate, eighteen and seventeen, and two boys, John and Matthew, fourteen and twelve. Both of us were born in Winnipeg and had moved to Stratford five years earlier when Bill became general manager of the Stratford Festival Theatre. We had a split-level house with a swimming pool in the back yard, a Bassett hound, a cat, a tank full of tropical fish, friends and fun and a future. A nice life.

It changed in a twinkling, as they say, when I turned around and saw his head on the coffee table. He was dead then, though I didn't know it. I gave him mouth-to-mouth resuscitation, but asked my daughter to take over, because I thought I must be doing it wrong. There was no response. It was too late. No second chances.

There is a kind of glory in sudden death: to go down at the peak of one's powers with both achievement and potential untarnished, all flags flying. The light is snapped off before it has had a chance to dim or fade. One giant step into the next world. But O pity the survivors! Mid-stride dying is very hard on them. They are left to face the overdue library books, the bouncing checks (party deceased, funds frozen), the work-in-progress, the plans underway, the gifts on order, all the machinery of daily life that was in full production and that has suddenly stopped. No time to slow down, to re-tool, to lay off. No time to prepare.

There is an Anglican prayer that reads in part, "Preserve us from sudden death." It's a point well taken. Because sudden death does throw a terrible rock into the machinery of normal family living.

No more so, really, than the terrible agony of a terminal illness. That's the way my father went, with cancer, so I've had the dubious privilege of seeing it both ways. It is painful to watch helplessly while someone you love slips away from you. I watched my mother be the eyes and ears and hands of the world her husband was leaving, caring for him with a zeal that almost put her to bed, too. Swift, or agonizingly slow, when death strikes a family, life will never be the same.

Mercifully, one does not immediately realize that fact, however death arrives. First things first. And the first thing on the agenda is a funeral. Funerals are primitive. I always thought so and nothing has changed my mind. And yet, as one friend pointed out, they fulfill the necessary function of convincing everyone that the worst has really happened; he really is dead. And it gives the peripheral friends a chance to do their duty, nevermore to be seen. It's called "paying their respects," and I suppose that fulfills a need as well. Tradition and custom can carry one through an awful lot of swampy territory.

One of the dangers for the widow, though, is that it is done all too swiftly. Speed is not necessarily a good thing. Well-meaning friends are anxious to get everything done, arranged, finished, so that you can start getting over it. You don't ever get over it. Loss is permanent. Part of you has died, too. So a little wallowing at this time doesn't hurt, if people would only allow it. But our society seems to demand that we behave ourselves at funerals, and after. And we do. Deportment is all. Breakdowns are bad form. But a

3

little howling at the moon might save a lot of tension later on.

One week after my husband's death I was alone with my children. It takes about the same length of time to be left alone with a new baby to bring up. In the latter case, nerves are offset by joy and anticipation. In the silence following the frenzied activity of funeral arrangements and people dropping in, the sad fact begins to sink in: life will never be the same again. You are definitely alone. With a lot to learn. As one friend put it: it took me twenty years to learn to live with my husband; I wasn't going to unlearn overnight. Neither will you.

Mourning is a natural and necessary process. It shouldn't be rushed. For in grieving over the loss of another, what we are really doing is grieving over our loss of self, all the self that was invested in that person. We have to get it back somehow.

Freud said that the bereaved has to withdraw her emotional attachment from the deceased. "Withdraw the libido," he said, and, at the same time, begin to "internalize the lost love object." That means letting go, letting go of your husband, without losing your memories of him. You have to build a new relationship with him, and you have to become a new you. It takes time. It can't be hurried.

Grief is an illness with recognizable symptoms. Loss of sleep and loss of appetite contribute effectively to a general exhaustion. There may be headaches, stomachaches, bowel upsets, perhaps even a rash as a result of tension. A dreadful apathy can overtake you, and a withdrawal from reality. Sometimes you can see, more often hear, your husband in another room. For weeks after Bill died I could hear the evening paper rustling as he turned the pages. You lose contact with reality; you lose your trust in life. Death seems much simpler than life and much more welcome. One widow wrote, "I remember I used to think each night as I said my prayers that I was one day nearer the end of my life—and glad of it. That feeling left me."

Note that. The feeling left her. It does, you know. Bereavement is a terrible mental wound, slow to heal, but it does heal. It just takes time. Terrible cliché and not quite true. It also takes hard work. It isn't going to go away all by itself. You have to work at it.

Life, as my oldest daughter said to me, suddenly becomes an uncharted adventure. I found that hard to understand when she said it. I resented it and pushed it away from me. I had been content with my life as it had been, known and charted and secure and happy as it was. Why should I be comforted by the promise of unknown hazards and adventures? And yet, now I see what she meant. How did she know so much?

In his strange and wonderful book *Living Your Dying*, Stanley Keleman hints at the same idea. "Endings," he writes, "bring us face to face with the unknown. Endings force us to make new relationships, or at least offer that opportunity. . . . Many people will say 'that person is irreplaceable to me.' The truth of the matter is that making an ending forces us to start being more self-reliant, or at least offers that opportunity."

No one ever told you it was an opportunity before.

❋2
From grief to joy

> *Joy does not mean riotous glee but it does mean the purposive employment of energy in a self-chosen enterprise. It does mean pride and self-confidence. It does mean communication and co-operation with others, based on delight in their company and your own . . . to have something to desire, to make, to achieve, and at last something genuine to give.*
>
> GERMAINE GREER

In a death-denying society like ours, the crisis of bereavement is a tough one to face, because no one wants to let you face it, and no one wants to share it either.

"Cheer up," people say. "You have your children." Or your memories, or your health, or your money. But your husband is gone.

"Pull yourself together," they say. "There are worse things than death." They're right, of course, but name one.

"Stiff upper lip," they say. "He wouldn't want to see you like this." What's so bad about a quivering lower one? I'd like there to be a little breast-beating when I go, just to let me know I was missed.

"Carry on," they say. "You have to get up and keep going." Why?

In all other cases of shock, we are told the recommended treatment is rest and warmth. Pile on the blankets and the comfort. Why should it be any different for the shock of death? An electric blanket may be a poor substitute for a husband, but at a time like this it's the closest thing to the womb there is—a place to retreat to and lick one's wounds.

Psychologists have only recently recognized the deep needs of the survivor, and the patterns that grief must take if one is to recover and go on living a meaningful life. The whole process is described as "grief work," and it is very hard work. No part of it can be shirked. If it is, it will have to be faced and gone through at a later date, often with severe complications. After the initial, blessed numbness has worn off, there are hostility and guilt and depression to be worked through before any acceptance can be achieved.

Roughly classified, the stages of grief may be described as shock, denial, and acceptance, but a more detailed analysis may prove to be of some value. You'll find a number of variations depending on whose book you read, but here is a fairly comprehensive list:

I Shock
  1. Initial shock
  2. Emotional release
  3. Loneliness

II Denial
  1. Depression
  2. Panic
  3. Hostility
  4. Guilt
  5. Inability to return to normal
     activity

III Acceptance
  1. Gradual hope
  2. Struggle to affirm reality

The whole process can take well over a year, and there is always the chance after that of an unpredictable relapse when some unexpected, heartbreakingly simple commonplace suddenly reduces you to helpless tears. Bear with it. These symptoms do not necessarily follow the order of my neat column, nor does everyone suffer all of them. But they may serve as a guide to the kinds of emotions a widow must work through to earn her wings (not angel wings—wings of hope). The comfort in confronting such a list is the realization that you are not alone. Others have gone this path before you as there will be others after you. I know. I've been that way myself.

The psychiatrist Dr. Thomas Holmes has listed those life events that cause stress in human beings, with a stress-rating for each event. The event with the highest number of stress points is the death of a spouse, with a box score of 100; next on the list is divorce, with a score of 75. Holmes's idea is that no one should accumulate a life stress score of more than 200 in any given twelve-month period. A higher score can lead to serious illness, injury, or accidents. This is why one of the best pieces of advice a recent widow can listen to is: "Don't do anything rash."

Even if she doesn't do anything, there are changes that accompany the loss of her husband which automatically add to her stress. A change in financial status carries a score of 38; her finances have automatically undergone a change, and she won't be certain how she's fixed for a few months. Change to a different line of work is worth 36 points, or a business readjustment is 39. Within the year, if she wasn't working before, it's likely she will start now. If she was working, there are still subtle differences: she is the sole breadwinner now and it changes the job as well as the person doing it. A change in work responsibility is worth 29. Changes in eating (15) and sleeping habits (16) also account for stress points, and these changes are impossible to avoid.

One widow assured me it would be six months before I would be able to taste food or sleep through the night. Another one, older, said it would be a year. I wouldn't say my sleeping habits have ever recovered.

I was always the last one to bed. Bill was the one who locked the doors, put the milk order out and the cat in the basement, and turned out the lights around me until I said, "Hey, wait for me!" Now I try, I do try, to get to bed at a reasonable hour—and then I write in bed. But if something happens to hook me, like a book, or a list, or a new idea, it's game over. I'm up till 3 or 4 A.M. and sleep seems a waste of time.

A change in social life also causes stress (18 points), and it's more than that. As you get cut out of the social stream, resentment increases, and that brings a stress of its own. Special events, even happy ones, bring stress to everyone. Christmas carries a score of 12, and the first one A.D. must carry a little more than that. In these stressful times, it's not hard to pile up a sizable score even without a Super Event to send it soaring. Each family has its own events which will add to the strain. My first child left home to go off to university within that first year—that's 29 points. One divorcée asked me what was the score if your oldest unmarried daughter had an abortion. Holmes didn't cover that one. You can see that even if you don't do anything, you have enough stress to work through without going out of your way to find some more.

That's why I say for at least a year, sit tight. Work through your grief. Don't add moving or other major changes to the already drastic change in your life, if you can possibly help it.

You have a lot of emotions, reflexes, and habits tied up in one person, and they have to be released before you go on. A friend of mine, Mary Vachon, who is a mental health consultant (with a PhD in death and dying), describes your task in this way: "You have to get back a lot of the emotion you invest in the dead person." She also says that the 32 percent widowed under the age of sixty-five are the worst problem area; that is, they represent a high-risk group.

Research has been carried out in test groups across the country to determine the effectiveness of one-on-one self-help widow groups, inspired by the initial efforts conducted at Harvard University. In such a group that Mary Vachon worked with, she found that in the year following the death of their husbands, the young widows studied experienced three times as many hospital admissions as other women of similar age. The widows studied experienced a 12 percent increase in mortality during the first year of bereavement. And 32 percent of widows suffer "marked deterioration in health" within thirteen months after their husband's death, compared to 2 percent for a control group.

Mary Vachon listed the types of cases with the greatest risk factor:

1. those with poor social support;
2. those under forty-five whose husbands died suddenly; or, conversely, those over sixty-five, whose husbands suffered a lingering death;
3. those with an ambivalent relationship to the deceased (those who have the most difficulty recovering are those who had the worst marriages);
4. those who were denied the grief experience because of minimal funeral ceremonies;
5. those with previous psychiatric difficulties. (If they were suicidal before, their chances of death by suicide are greatly increased; suicide is a high risk for the first five years following a spouse's death.)

Like most widows I know, I behaved myself during the initial impact. I had an ulcer that did tend to stand at attention under stress, though, so my doctor deemed it advisable to give me a relaxant to keep my gut from taking me on an acid trip. It was mild, however, and used sparingly. I was fully aware of what I was doing and why. I have since heard of widows whose doctors thought they were doing them a favor by tranquilizing them out of their skulls during the first after-days of shock. I do not believe in such a practice, trying to turn a pill into a twentieth-century balm of Gilead. Nor do I believe in the indiscriminate use of sleeping pills. If you are fortunate enough to have a religious faith, you will find that prayer does much more than Nembutal.

One widow told me, "My electric blanket saved me." Me too. I used to turn it and the bedside lamp on long before bedtime so that when I was finally ready to try to sleep, the light and warmth would welcome me. Sleep does return in time, though perhaps your sleep patterns will have changed. All your other patterns will have changed; why should sleep be different?

Use the time. Other widows besides me—and not necessarily writers—have used paper in the wee small hours of the night to keep them company and sane. With me it began with my sympathy letters—some seven hundred of them. I wrote long into the night, every night, for weeks and weeks, replying at length to each letter I had received. This, of course, kept me from facing that empty (but warm) bed.

I began to keep a diary every night. It was a substitute for my bedtime conversation with Bill. It also proved to be a wonderful release (note stage 2 in the list of recovery symptoms above). Emotional release comes in many different forms. Welcome them all, because you need them. Paper helps dry the tears. Tears will come, of course, and must not be denied. But sometimes, when the pain is too overwhelming, it helps to distance it a little, or at least set it slightly aside, by writing down what you feel.

I didn't always wait till bedtime. If something really got to me, I'd rush to my diary and write it all down. A lot of the early pages are tear-splattered, but ball-point pens don't run. I think it's better to run to paper than to a tranquilizer. In my case it's almost as addictive, but there are fewer side effects.

I have since recommended a journal to a number of people, not necessarily widows, who were depressed. "Write it down," I say. "Get it on paper, and take a look at it." All who have tried it report that it helps. That's what those *Nothing Books* are for. Have you seen them? They are bound books of blank paper, no dates, nothing, just blank paper; much better than a page-a-day, dated diary with an imitation leather cover and a tinny lock and key—that's for teeny-boppers. If you can't afford the hardcover edition, there's a paperback *Nothing Book* on the market now. If, like me, you tend to write uphill and need lines, then get yourself a school scribbler. The important thing is to have a special notebook for your writing, and let it happen.

It's not only grief you may want to express. If you do get angry or resentful at people's treatment of you, at real or fancied slights, you can write it all down, let off all your steam, without saying anything you might be sorry for later. If, like me, you are a this-time-last-year kind of person, you can indulge in that to your heart's content, without boring anyone. Go ahead and dwell on your milestones. Recall—and write down—the happy times as well as the bad ones. Set yourself assignments. Thanksgiving is a good place to start. Each Thanksgiving I make a point of thinking of and writing down all the things I have to be thankful for. Work at it. Don't take anything for granted. Realize how blessed you are, and count your blessings by writing them down. Then, later, on a day when you've hit a low ebb, go back and read what you've written. That will help. You have just become your own therapist. Never underestimate the power of paper! Consider your diary your Withdrawal Book. And don't worry if you can't spell; no one's going to see it but you. Paper is about to become your best friend, as it is mine.

"How frighteningly few are the persons whose death would spoil our appetite and make the world seem empty," wrote the San Francisco philosopher Eric Hoffer, and it's a good thing. You wouldn't wish this on anyone.

"Ah, but you're strong," people say—have they said that to you? "You'll survive." I decided then that if I'm ever re-incarnated, I'm going to come back pure marshmallow. In the meantime, people were right. I am strong—one of the clichés that happens to be true—because I have this other friend called God without Whom I am nothing. The harder I lean on Him, the more I pray and the more I am open, so in direct proportion the more I gain support, comfort, and strength. When I falter still, when pain overwhelms me, as it still can, it is because I haven't turned to Him enough, haven't opened enough.

A friend of mine was in the hospital for a cracked vertebra and she was suffering muscle spasms. She was told not to fight them, to ride with them instead and let each spasm run its course. So with this pain of parting, I had to open my heart and let the pain come all the way in—and keep on going until it comes out the other side. Sometimes you feel as if it's on a circular track; it keeps coming around again. Finally, though, you will be not whole again but healed.

I do not rage. I do not question. I praise God and thank Him and ask for help. And I get it. In abundance, as they say.

It's hard sometimes to distinguish between genuine grief and self-pity. "Our tears are selfish," wrote Peter Marshall in his book of sermons, *Mr. Jones, Meet the Master,* "for we are self-centered—self-absorbed. We keep thinking of what it means to us. We reflect how much we miss the departed, and we weep because we begrudge their going. We wish they had stayed on with us awhile. . . . We wish things had gone on as they were. We resent the change, somehow, never thinking what it must mean to them that are gone."

Self-pity is a kind of permissive self-dramatization. And grief is very like fear. "Perhaps," says C. S. Lewis, "more strictly, like suspense. Or like waiting; just hanging about waiting for something to happen. It gives life a permanently provisional feeling." Grief is an agonized apprehension of something that has already happened. It's standing at the edge of a void, a very recently carved hole that has forced a change in your direction. It is knowing, with a sinking feeling in your gut, that you have to go on, alone, and that's painful.

Pain takes many different forms. If you can let self-pity

give way to irony, there's hope for you yet. One of my children gave me the best example to follow. John, at fourteen, went off to his beloved summer camp as planned. One night at camp a group of boys was sitting around a campfire talking, John told me later, and they began to compare notes on their fathers' occupations. "What does your Dad do?" John had no intention of telling them his father had died two months before; that would involve a singling-out he didn't want. When it came his turn to say what his father did, he said casually, "Well, he lies around a lot."

I remember my refusal of a gift of lilacs the first spring A.D. because my husband was allergic to them. It took me weeks to stop heading for the passenger side of the car, and over two years before I ever spread out in the double bed—there was a small neat dent where I carefully slept on my side, though I always turned on the blanket on his side, in case a stray leg got chilled in the night. The first roast I attempted to carve caused a few tears and some messy chunks of meat. Fortunately, roast beef is so expensive now we don't have the problem very often. It is not, in fact, for the predictably difficult situations that you must brace yourself but for the simple events that can undo you. I was visiting friends and saw the wife slip a lipstick in her husband's pocket—all the preparation she needed to go out, since he had the money, identification, car and house keys. I used to do that too, and I can't anymore. That hurt. But these are examples of self-pity—easy traps—and not to be tolerated.

The panic associated with the depression of loneliness (see list again) seems to come when you are expected to do something you have always let your husband do because he did it so much better. We women have all been pampered and protected into a state of near-incompetence. If feminism gives women a stronger sense of self, a larger competence in financial and mechanical matters, a greater confidence in their own ability to cope with life's practical problems, then it will ease the role of widows everywhere. The first time I had to back into a parking place in a car park I realized anew that I was alone. There was no one to do it for me; I had to do it myself. I did, of course. Out of that initial panic rose determination and, eventually, skill. Now I can squeeze back into spaces that you wouldn't believe.

And then you hit another aspect of the loneliness. When you do achieve something, you have no one to share it with. Your loving reflector is gone. As one widower put it to me, "I know well the temptations of self-pity and the danger of enjoying sympathy. These come, I think, because that special understanding, so generously given and so esteeming, has abruptly gone, and there remains a struggle not to shrink and become less of a person. Widow and widower are so terribly vulnerable."

Depression is a form of anger. The loss of a loved one generates a lot of hostility which must be worked through. Often the hostility is directed at the person who died. The widow feels she has been unfairly abandoned, and it's all his fault. All the if-onlies are his fault. I know one widow who told me that every time she hit a crisis during the first year following her husband's death she'd address him aloud: "John Smith," she'd shout, "why did you leave me to face this alone?"

If the marriage was less than ideal, a terrible guilt accompanies the anger. The survivor feels guilty that she wasn't nicer, more patient, more forgiving, more loving. Whatever faults her spouse threw at her in their bad scenes, she hurls at herself with a cruel ferocity. Fine. Let it all happen. All those emotions have to be recovered and worked out.

Psychiatrist Karen Horney dealt with anger; she pointed out that we cannot deal with our anger unless we allow it to enter our consciousness. You have to recognize it and you mustn't be afraid of it. Maturity isn't denying anger; it's facing it. Repressing anger is dangerous, as is repressing grief. You have been deeply wounded, and you must act before gangrene sets in.

Anger is caused by some frustration—in this case, your

husband's death—which has thwarted your hopes and plans for a future that included him in it. If you're not angry at him, then you turn your anger on others for frustrating you: for ignoring you, you think; for forgetting you; for not making a fuss over you; for excluding you; in short, for going on living their own lives.

To rid yourself of anger you must either remove the obstacles in the path of your frustration or recognize what these obstacles are and change your expectations. Well, you can't remove the death. But you can recognize the gap between your expectations and people's performance, and do one or several things about that.

1. Close the gap. Be more realistic in your expectations. Realistic, not cynical.
2. In the case of genuine slights, rebuffs, or disappointments, shrug your shoulders and give up. Write them off. It happens. "I've lost the Soanso's," I moaned to a friend. "No," my friend said, "they've lost you."
3. Concentrate on the goodies. Play the Glad Game. Marvel at the unlooked-for, unexpected kindnesses people have done you. Say it out loud. Write it down. Count your blessings. Keep counting.
4. When you cannot remove the cause of your anger, when it's permanent, as in this case, then find extra energy in yourself to cope with it. Direct that energy into a creative, satisfying outlet: a sport, a hobby, a volunteer job, a new project at work. Make your anger-energy work for you!

Some people get angry at God. But as one widow told me, "I think He's big enough to handle it."

In my case, I felt neither hostility nor guilt. My husband

died such a sudden, freakish death that I could hardly blame him for leaving. He must have been as astonished as I was. And our marriage was so satisfying that it left nothing unsaid or undone. I'd have liked years more of it, mind you, but it was complete. Sometimes I now think, maybe we had it all and that's why it ended. Who knows? But my depression did turn into anger. I was angry at most of my friends. I demanded more of them than anyone could possibly deliver, and since people don't deliver much to widows, there was quite a gap between their delivery and my expectations. If only we could tell people the kind of help we need and expect.

At first we need someone to talk to, to pour it all out at, to go over the details of our life and his death until we have it all together and begin to accept it as reality and not some nightmare we may eventually waken from.

Next, we need someone to count on, some semblance of routine. Activity really does help, and widows left with children at home are fortunate in the sense that they have people they must do something for. A friend can, however, offer a regular visit or a planned activity to look forward to and count on for a few weeks or months.

A friend can also help with that next phase in our little list: inability to return to normal activity. It was a good friend who made me return to our weekly swimming class at the Y, and who made me have our annual swimming party at the end of the season. It was my own common sense that made me return to the church choir sooner than anyone else recommended.

When death has reduced "normal" to a meaningless word, any semblance of normal routine is a great help. Anything that gives you some kind of focus can help to keep you sane in those first terrible months of re-adjustment. That's why work can be a blessing. Gradually, unbidden, stray streamers of hope lighten the darkness. You know now it's not a case of getting over; it's getting through it.

Happiness is not a pursuit in itself and does not come on

command. Happiness is a by-product which sneaks up on you, unsought, when you're busy at something else. Joy, on the other hand, is a positive activity, one that is every person's duty to cultivate. I believe you must work at joy. Demand it as your right; pursue it as your goal; give it to others as your obligation to them.

One of the first things you can do, as you look around in your increasing light, is find someone else who needs help. One widow wrote me: "A source of strength is to either phone or go to see someone who is in far worse straits—and one does not have to look far." There are self-help programs operating here and there across the country, widows helping widows, and that's not a bad place to begin.

Only widows, or, if one is lucky, one's closest friends, can know what another widow is going through. It's a sisterhood with terrible dues, a membership you would avoid if you could. Once arrived, however, your capacity for compassion and sympathy and practical help expands enormously. Heart and hands reach out to help others in pain and need. And this, perhaps, is the greatest affirmation of reality a person can achieve.

✹3
Changing your lifestyle

The most difficult adjustment a woman is called on to make is learning to live alone after being married.

ISABELLA TAVES

A widow is not immediately aware of how different her life is. At first the changes seem minute. You go on in the house. You stick to the routine, especially if you have children. You do what must be done each day—cleaning, cooking, shopping. Familiar tasks are a blessing and a comfort. It's almost as if your husband were away on an extended business trip. Almost. There is less laundry, of course. The pressure of producing a great dinner every night, if you ever felt such a pressure, eases. Your social life drops like a stone.

The first thing you notice is that you have a lot more time on your hands. There is no one to coax you to have another cup of coffee, a drink, a chat, a walk. You seem to have become more efficient, but time hangs heavy. What do you want to save it for?

Little by little, though, the changes become more apparent and more drastic. It's as if the two of you had been arrows shot from two bows, your paths parallel. The event that stopped the flight of one arrow has deflected the path of yours. Little by little, the trajectory will be greatly changed. You're flying on alone. What happens, ultimately, is that your whole lifestyle changes.

This is a secret that your friends and acquaintances know before you do: you are a different person. External circumstances are going to force changes in you that you never expected. It's irrelevant whether or not you wanted them; they're going to happen. Life has written you a new script.

Since your future has changed so much, you might as well get ready for it by taking a long hard look at your life right now. Everything you have been accustomed to doing bears scrutiny and reevaluation. Start by questioning your daily routine. Why are you doing what you do in the way that you do it? Habit? Or necessity? For whom are you running your household now? What are your priorities?

You were probably running the house for your husband before. Dinner was set in accordance with the time he came home. Your shopping and free time were arranged to accommodate your social life together. If you worked as well, then you had, no doubt, reciprocal arrangements and divisions of labor, but it was team work. Everything you did was done with someone else's needs in mind. Marriage, we are told, is supposed to be an equal partnership, but some partnerships are more equal than others. And in most cases the older the widow, the more male-dominated the household was. Most marriages in this century and on this continent have acknowledged the male as the head of the household. Life With Father is a twentieth-century truism.

Now that Father isn't there, it's time you took a good look at yourself. Otherwise you're going to atrophy like Queen Victoria. Everyone knows the story of her devoted grief, how the room was kept as it always was, and Albert's clothes laid out every day. No one expects or admires that kind of paralysis on the part of a widow today.

Speaking of clothes, you should remove your husband's clothes from the house as soon as possible. It is more important that he take a permanent place in your heart and memory than be revered in a moth-eaten sweater. I gave shirts to nephews, underwear and socks and pajamas to the Salvation Army, and sold the good suits to a second-hand clothing store. The beautiful ties that my husband collected and prized I gave away to his closest men friends, to remember him by, at least as long as they were in style. Empty the closet and open your heart.

And stay open. You're going to have to keep an open mind if you're going to change, and you have to change, though slowly at first. Little by little you realize you don't have to cater to other people's needs all the time; in fact, it's time you started paying some attention to your own. You're the only one who's going to.

And that's the next step to total assessment. You begin to take a look at all your habits, and you start to analyze how you got that way, why you do this or that, and you begin to question the necessity of continuing in the same—not pattern—rut.

The first changes are the hardest and the most exciting— even simple ones like shifting shopping times or your laundry habits. Your cooking habits change, too, and not always for the better. The widow living alone has the biggest problem in the kitchen. I read recently that a single person pays at least 10 percent more for food because of the inability to buy in quantity at lower prices. Even one tin of something lasts two or three meals, and boredom sets in, accompanied by a lack of appetite. My father, a doctor, used to say that women living alone subsisted on a diet of tea and toast and cornflakes—"No fit food," he used to say, "for growing females." The widow living alone should try to maintain good eating habits to ensure her health. If that sounds too preachy, I'm sorry. But you have a long time to go on alone; you might as well do it in good health.

One of the hidden bonuses of being single is that you are in control. You make the decisions now, so don't be afraid to experiment. Why not have soup for breakfast (I like cream soup best), or a gigantic baked potato loaded with butter or sour cream (but nothing else except maybe a salad) for dinner? Make a point, if you can afford it, of having a guest at least once a week, for lunch or dinner, or for coffee and dessert. It's not only good for your morale and your appetite, but if you choose your guest wisely, it will also result in a return invitation, which is even better for the morale and the appetite.

Cooking presents different problems to the working mother, to the scrimping housewidow, and to the lonely, older widow. Each situation, however, is sure to be different from what it was before. As a working mother you have to be sure your children are getting the best nutrition possible with the least amount of effort and maximum efficiency on your part. Obviously, you can't spend hours in the kitchen fussing about food. At the same time, you can't simply broil a fast chop every night. That's too expensive, and dull. There never has been a time when more information was available for whatever problem has to be handled. The libraries and bookstores are crammed with cookbooks, and there are a lot of them dedicated to casseroles, do-ahead foods, the specific problems of a working cook, or cooking for one or two. Similarly, if money is a problem—and when isn't it?—there are cookbooks that tell you how to get the most nutrition, fun, and good taste for your food dollars.

Surveys have indicated that women without men do not set as good a table as they did. The image you had of yourself as Earth Mother, Hostess Bountiful, Giver of All Good Things to Eat, seems to have disappeared. The reasons are understandable enough. You don't have the same incentive that you did. You've lost your most appreciative audience. You don't have as much money. Lots of reasons. Old Mother Hubbard's cupboard was bare—it's obvious she was a widow.

This change is almost imperceptible as it happens; it creeps up on you by degrees. As a matter of fact, until I moved, I kept on running a household for six, even though two and then three of the occupants were no longer with us. My oldest daughter went off to university the fall after my husband died, followed by my second daughter the year after. I had three fridges and a freezer, and I seemed to keep on filling them, though I must admit I had more trouble emptying them than before. It wasn't until I was in a three-bedroom apartment with one refrigerator that I began buying and cooking for three instead of six, and that's when I found I couldn't always have an extra one or two for dinner on short notice. Of course, that wasn't the only reason. My typewriter, by that time, was far more important to me than my kitchen. You see, changes sneak up on you, whether you are aware of them or not.

The way you spend your time changes more than the way you set your table. The absence of your husband changes the way you spend almost every moment of your life, especially the moments you used to spend together. Times when you are most empty and unoccupied, like the hour before dinner when he used to come home and talk over the day, or Saturday night, which you used to spend together—these are the very times when your married friends are busiest with their husbands. You must fill that time for yourself.

The dinner hour is the easiest to fill. You simply move it forward; you don't have to wait for anyone to come home, and kids are always happy to eat early. It gives you a longer evening, but you'll learn to fill that productively, and even be grateful for the time. If you're working, there's less problem with empty times on weekdays. You'll be too busy to notice when you have to do everything yourself.

I know a lot of widows who write letters, pay their bills, and balance their budgets on Saturday nights. Other nights it is possible to find single things to do—meetings to go to, activities to occupy yourself—but Saturday seems to be couple-oriented, like the society we live in. If you want to be occupied on Saturday night, you're going to have to plan ahead. As a matter of fact, all singles have to do a great deal of planning ahead. You don't have a built-in companion for whatever spontaneous activity comes to mind.

I have on occasion gone out to dinner on a Saturday night with a wrench of widows, but I don't recommend this as common practice. Tickets for many events are more expensive on Saturdays, and restaurants are usually more crowded. It doesn't matter that there are five or six of you, if you're all female, the waiter says, "Oh, you're alone," and puts you near the kitchen door. Get a *TV Guide* or buy some pretty stationery and a new address book and brush up on your correspondence instead.

Sunday is white-knuckle day. It helps to go to church, if you are that way inclined (I am). Some working mothers find it helps to sleep in. If you're a working mother you may be doing the laundry or other household chores on Sunday afternoon. This is often more productive and less depressing than a walk. Walking is best with two.

For a while I tried to fill Sundays by having guests for dinner, either whole families that my children would enjoy, or singles that they could help to entertain. It gave us all a focus, I thought, to concentrate on someone outside ourselves on Sunday afternoon. It helps—for a while. If you have been accustomed to cooking a good Sunday dinner, you won't feel the pressure of having "company" as much. If you look around, you can find any number of waifs and strays who would enjoy a Sunday dinner. There are lots of singles around who are as lonely as you are. In fact, singles are better than families. You don't expect them to reciprocate.

After one season I quit having people for Sunday dinner. No one ever asked us back—that's how it gradually dawned on me that my friends had changed. Don't dwell on it when it happens to you. Accept what has happened and move on. Anyway, company for Sunday dinner became less and less attractive because (a) it's expensive and (b) it's tiring. There are some weeks you just don't have the time or energy to make a special dessert.

24

You will find, as time goes by, that the people you have over and the people who invite you to their homes differ from the people you used to see when you were part of a couple. That's the way it goes. You are a different person now, and you're not the only one who has learned how different you are. One plus one equaled a couple before, and you and your husband moved easily among a group of friends who considered you a unit. Like Mutt and Jeff. Ham and eggs. But in the eyes of the world, or at least of the society you live in, two take away one doesn't equal one. Most of the time it equals nothing. Face it: you are odd woman out. Very few people want seven or nine or eleven, let alone thirteen, at their dinner tables. Most people think you'd rather not come alone to their parties. They think tickets come in even numbers.

The remarkable thing is that other people change faster than you do. You still cling to the idea that you are a person, a human being in your own right. No one else does. You are going to have to change their minds for them, and in the process you will undergo a few changes yourself.

Never mind. If you're forgotten when it comes to playtime, you're Number One on the list when it comes to work—unpaid, of course. I mean, you have all that time on your hands. The first fall after my husband's death I was not invited out to dinner but I was asked to run a publicity campaign for the local Y, bake pies for the church bake sale, sell books for the Y book sale, canvass for the United Way, be an area manager for a fund-raising drive, and fill in on short notice as a fourth at bridge. I hate bridge.

Maybe what people do to you actually helps while it hurts. It hurts at the time but you begin to learn the hard way that you really are alone. As my first Christmas A.D. approached, one of my closest friends said to me, "I'd invite you all for dinner on Christmas but you have to face reality sooner or later." I thought I had been facing reality for six months, daily. Suttee, the practice whereby the widow throws herself on her husband's funeral pyre, has been outlawed in India. We still practice a subtle form of it; you die by inches, of loneliness.

If you think I'm being too bitter or grim or harsh, bear with me. I'm stating the facts first, in their plainest terms. There are, of course, wonderful exceptions, sources of help and comfort you never expected—and often not from the friends you have relied on over the years. A drastic change has occurred in your life, and it sets off a chain reaction of changes all the way down the line, in friends and family and society, as well as in your whole lifestyle.

Well, that's as bad as it gets. From here on in, you have nowhere to go but up. It's a long climb, but you have lots of time, and you have an asset no one, maybe not even you, realizes. Yourself. If you weren't before, you are about to become your own best friend.

Having told you the worst, let me now reassure you. There never has been a time in history when it has been more exciting to be a single woman. The feminist movement is only a few years old, but it has already loosened some of the codes and paved the way for a single woman to make a new life for herself as a vital, functioning, contributing person. It is still up to you, of course, but others have stuck their feet in doors for you. The future is yours in a way that it never has been before. Whether you find that challenging or frightening depends on you.

If friends invite you somewhere—anywhere!—say yes. Don't give them the excuse not to ask you next time because "you'd only say no anyway." They find their own reasons quickly enough. If you're working and there's an office party, go to it. You may end up on sandwich detail or the punch bowl, but go. If you're invited to a wedding and you have no one to go with, go anyway—and that goes for cocktail and any other kinds of parties, dinners, theater performances, home-and-school or annual meetings, political rallies, anything. Go! You will find you have to draw some lines at volunteer work, because the invitations in this area are endless. You need to decide where you will devote your energy and time and where your saturation point is, because it's in you, not in the work to be done.

One of the things I didn't know I knew, I learned from my widowed mother and aunts, whom I had unconsciously observed before I became a widow myself. I watched these widows say no and dwindle. Mind you, they were a lot older than I was, and it was harder for them to say yes. Saying yes means making an effort, spending some energy, and maybe even some money, and taking risks. So my motto as a widow is: "Never say no to anything—within reason!" I have ended up in some peculiar situations because of this, and I have had some rotten times. But I have also had some unexpectedly good times and met a few really enjoyable people I might not otherwise have met. As a newly single person, you have to keep meeting new people, you see, because a lot of your old relationships are no longer valid. You are the one who's changing, though it seems at first that other people have.

Some friends may forget you at the dinner table, but I have found that a single woman is far more welcome as a house guest than a couple. A single woman can fit in the spare room, help with the kids, pitch in with the cooking, and adapt to any plans going on in a busy, active household far more readily than a couple.

Travel is a wonderful form of escape. Every widow I know will go anywhere at the drop of a hat or a ticket. I have never refused any trip or visit that is offered me and I have been the grateful recipient of food, drink, hospitality, and even airline tickets from dear, kind, generous friends.

I still feel alien on this planet without my husband. Somehow, when I am away from home, I feel less strange, in a perverse sort of way. I mean, I'd be foreign anyway. And I like the feeling of being suspended in space and time, of having, for the time being, no real responsibilities, no commitments, no pressures. So often, since Bill died, I have asked myself in wonder, "What am I doing here?" When I'm on a trip I know the answer. I'm visiting.

So I have traveled a lot since his death and rarely stay in hotel rooms. I have learned how to be a guest, and I have become closer friends with my long-distance friends and their children than I might ever have had the opportunity to be otherwise.

I like flying alone. I like driving alone. But I find that I cannot get used to going to the movies or the theater alone. Everyone has his threshold of intolerance, and this seems to be mine. I have done it, but I don't like it. I have sought a few friends, those with busy husbands or none at all, who like movies as much as I do, and I go with them. Or else I go with my boys, which limits the choice of movie these days. I am more aggressive about the theater. I get myself a single ticket and offer dinner before or drinks and supper after to a couple I know is also going. Or I get two or three tickets and offer myself as a package deal. This usually results in dinner on the man or the couple. The point is that anything is possible; you just have to plan a little more. One single complained to me that life had become once again one long series of dates.

It's true. You have to plan ahead. It takes money and time and energy to maintain a social life, and all three have decreased for the widow. It's a whole new ballgame, and it requires a whole new set of ground rules. You start by trying to fill in lonely gaps—the dinner hour, Saturday nights, Sundays. You progress to theater-going, travel, new interests, maybe even, in time, new men. But we'll get to that later.

Brace yourself. You have to develop a single psyche again. As one friend said to me, "Just remember you're not married anymore." It's painful, but it bears repeating, because after all these years of marriage, it's hard to remember.

As you go on, you see, the changes get both easier and more drastic. You change your emphasis. You realize that people are more important than things, that your children are more important than your routine, that you are more important than conventional habits.

Habit is a comfortable skin that cushions a lot of shocks. Shedding the skin can be painful. Change is always painful. But you have had the biggest change of your life thrust upon you. No choice. If you don't change to meet it, you won't survive.

❀4
Coping with money

> *Money may not be important but it quiets the nerves.*
>
> JOE E. LEWIS

Before my husband died my two chief problems in life were (1) how to find more time to write and (2) how to lose weight. Now they are much more basic: sex and money. I don't know whether that represents progress or not.

"Sex," according to a contemporary greeting card, "is like money. When you don't have it, it's hard to think of anything else." Widows think about both a lot. This chapter is about money.

It's called instant cut-off when a death occurs. Banks know before your distant relatives that your husband has died, and the checks and bills come trailing back along with the first sympathy card: "Party deceased; funds frozen." In the case of a joint account, you won't have this problem. The bank often doesn't know that anything has changed, until you tell it.

Even though you may not feel like eating, you and your family have to be fed. Even if you are alone, expenses go on and must be met. Even if you have been handling the household accounts, it's different when you're alone with them. Even if you have been working all along, you are still missing one income, usually the larger one. All this must be allowed for. And you have to keep oiling the ongoing machinery of life with money even while you are coping with the wrench that has been thrown into it.

One dear friend, who happened to be in the insurance business, came to me four or five days after Bill died and tactfully drew me aside.

"Betty Jane," he said, "if you need money, I can lend you two dollars."

Such a gentle joke, such a delicate way of telling me I could borrow money if I needed it. I hope you have such a friend.

What do you do after the bomb has fallen but before the smoke has cleared? Well, did you know that you can get an instant cash advance on your husband's life insurance policy? Most life insurance agents pride themselves on the efficiency and speed with which they settle a claim. If you need help, don't hesitate to ask for it.

Either way, with an advance or a swift settlement, there is instant money available to settle hospital and doctors' bills, pay funeral expenses, and clean up the outstanding bills remaining from a life in progress. I was fortunate, because I received a generous death benefit from my husband's employers. Financial panic didn't set in for two or three months. But there is usually a death benefit paid to a widow. Go to your husband's employer and inquire. If he's had more than one employer, check this out with his former employers as well. As always, it doesn't hurt to ask.

And use your insurance company. Not many people do, not enough. Surveys have shown that life insurance agents rank farther down on a list of widows' helpers than they should. Family, friends, and lawyers are above clergymen these days, but life insurance agents are low down on the list along with bankers and union representatives.

We had moved out of the city where our life insurance

agent lived, but he happened to be in our area at the time of my husband's death, so he and his wife drove down to see me and meet with my lawyer. He outlined what was available. His only advice to me was not to blow the money on a mink coat or a trip to Florida, and then he went away and I never heard from him again. His office sent my husband a birthday card two weeks later. I sent it back. (He apologized.)

Several years later, I told that story at an MDRT (Million Dollar Round Table) meeting I was invited to address. My friendly insurance agent was present but didn't get in touch with me then. Later I received a letter from him, with copies sent to key people in his own company and at MDRT, finally telling me his side of the story. He had, he said, offered explicit advice as to the disposal of the money, and on settlement options, none of which I heard or my lawyer paid attention to. He never heard from my lawyer again, and let it go.

I wrote back, explaining again what I have maintained all along, that no woman is in her right mind in the days and weeks following the death of her husband. She has an attention span of about three seconds, and the understanding of a bowl of Jell-O. She quivers, but she doesn't react. No one understands this.

Try to let people know that you can't think. We are so intent on preserving our decorum, on trying to act like grown-up human beings, that we fool a lot of people into thinking we are actually competent. It's just not so. When you don't understand what someone is telling you, say so. When you have forgotten what someone has told you, say that, too, and ask for a careful repetition, maybe even in writing. Usually it's your future they're talking about and attention must be paid, sooner or later. Preferably later.

So I'm telling you. Yelp a little. Sound off. You are not a little lone widow dependent on your meekness and other people's good will for casual handouts. You are a single (that hurts, but it's true) human being with all the rights thereto appertaining, and you'd be amazed at how many rights you have.

So holler for help. And one of the first places you should holler is at your life insurance company. I was assured, in the course of my research, that a widow can approach a life insurance company on her own, without a lawyer to hold her hand or guide her or speak for her.

"By all means," I was told, "get a lawyer and make your will—every widow should have a will—but when it comes to settling life insurance, you don't need a lawyer. You can do it all through your agent or the claims department."

Life insurance agents have frequently asked me since then how they can convince people that they do have the widow's best interests at heart, and that they frequently know better what to do with the money than an accountant or a lawyer. If you have some doubts or reservations, get several opinions, from your regular advisors and your insurance agent. Shop and compare, as they say. Don't be as ignorant and trusting as I was.

A great deal that I wasn't even aware of was done for me by my lawyer. I wasn't aware of very much at the time. Perhaps it was a crippling kindness, but who was I to question it? Mind you, I paid for it. I am not criticizing what was done for me. It had to be done, because I was helpless. I had never handled even household accounts before Bill died, and now I was busy trying to learn *everything*. And to think I had thought I was a reasonably intelligent, liberated woman! It is shameful that I should have been so incompetent. If the feminist movement does nothing else, perhaps it will raise women's consciousness to a level of simple competence. Mine wasn't.

After the smoke has cleared and the bills are paid, you have to take stock of your financial position and start making some plans for the future. Learn something else I didn't know, and save yourself some money. If you can afford to do it, roll your husband's IRA (Individual Retirement Account) money directly into an IRA of your own, rather than take it as income in one whopping taxable amount. You have to do this within sixty days. If you need some but not all of the money, you can take what you need, paying tax on that, and put the rest into an IRA. If you really have to take it all as a lump sum you can still get a tax-break called ten-year averaging. You can have it all in the year you take it, but you can be taxed over ten years for it, as if it were paid in ten equal payments. That's in addition to whatever other income you will be earning, which, of course, will also be taxed. You have to consider what you are going to do with the money and take a good hard look at interest rates (if you're thinking of investing it) before you decide. Get some help with this. Discuss it with a good tax advisor.

You normally don't get any money from an IRA until you are at least 59½ years old, or if you do, you pay a 10 percent penalty on it. You can keep on contributing to it until you're 70, if you're still earning income to do it. At 70, you must begin to take it out, at least 1/12 of it a year until the total amount is liquidated. Of course, this money is then taxable. If you don't need to use all of it, however, you may be able to find a way to invest it to keep on earning you some money.

There are more and more articles, books, and advice columns about money, and specifically about women and money, than there ever have been. I keep learning more all the time, and you will, too. As fast as the government keeps finding ways to keep us poor and to tax us on money we haven't got, we have to keep figuring out ways to make it and make it work for us. There aren't many loopholes left, for widows or anyone. It's a real challenge.

Ninety percent of working people have group life insurance. Virtually all group policies and many individual insurance policies have a disability waiver on them. If your husband had a prolonged terminal illness during which he was unable to work, it is possible that this clause on the policy will make premium payments unnecessary for the period of time he was disabled. If you were aware of it during the illness, it made for one less bill to pay. If you are not aware of it even now, ask. You may be entitled to a refund. Don't be afraid to ask. It might save you money, maybe even get you some back.

My father had arranged to buy a set of encyclopedias a few months before his terminal illness was diagnosed. My husband and I said we'd take over the payments and the books, because we had always wanted a set. A few months after my father's death I was going through some papers and found his contract with the book company. There was a clause that wiped out the payments in the event of the purchaser's death. I wrote the company and asked about this. They not only cleared the remaining payments; they reimbursed us for the payments we had made since my father's death. You see, it doesn't hurt to ask.

Widows are often not aware of the group insurance their husbands may have through their work. Today, about half of all life insurance policies are group insurance, and as I said, at least 90 percent of all employed people have group life insurance, so you should find out about it. Ask. Contact your husband's employer. Be sure to have your husband's Social Security number and his group insurance certificate handy. See if you can find the booklet describing the group benefits; it will have instructions on how to make the claim. (This is the time to ask about the disability premium waiver, too.) And while you're at it, ask about the pension fund, any accrued vacation or sick pay, terminal pay allowances, service recognition awards, unpaid commissions, credit union balance, whatever.

You might check the health insurance plan, too. If your husband was insured in a family plan with the company he worked for, that plan lasts for thirty days. You may have an opportunity to pay into it, too, and keep your protection, but be careful. The company is not obligated to do anything for you. It can give you a minimum coverage and charge you anything. You get no special treatment or price just because you're a widow. Again, you may have to shop around for a suitable medical insurance program for yourself. Who ever said anything was easy?

Frequently a long terminal illness can eat up all the insurance and savings and a widow faces financial as well as emotional disaster. In cases where there is severe debt, a financial planner must be called in to help solve the problem. Talk to your bank manager. Talk to a lawyer, relatives, business friends. Ask questions. Ask for help. People often want to help but don't know how. Show them. Ask them. The world seems very harsh and empty right now, but there are hands out there waiting to help you. Reach out to them if you need them.

I have been contacted by individual insurance agents across the country who want to know how they can help widows. They are all aware of how much more there is to a widow's future than the mere settling of a claim. And they all have this odd double image of themselves: the public image of the rapacious businessman betting on other people's lives, and their own sure knowledge of how necessary life insurance is and how much it helps. Anyway, many of them are more than willing to sit down and do some financial planning with a widow, and many of them are offering their services to widows' groups, seminars, and workshops. Find out what's going on in your community and get some help from these sympathetic experts in planning your future.

Which brings us up to right now. The moment of truth. How much is there to live on?

If you have been one of the fortunate competent women who handled your family's financial affairs, then you already know what it costs to run your household—correction: past tense—what it *did* cost. It is a sad and ironic fact that it will not cost as much. Husbands, bless them, are expensive. You not only have less food to prepare and less laundry to do; you also have less entertainment to pay for, fewer impulse purchases, and less drive to accumulate things. Yours is no longer an expanding economy; it is a shrinking one—an ironic blessing.

Anyway, perhaps you already have a budget and know where the money goes. If not, sit down with one. There is a booklet put out by the American Council of Life Insurance/Health Insurance Association of America that includes a twelve-month worksheet that will guide you in budgeting your fixed expenses, daily living expenses, and savings for the future. (We do keep talking about the future, don't we? Just when you thought you didn't have any left.) The booklet is called "The Money Manager: Step-by-Step to Money Management" and is available free of charge (for a single copy) from:

> American Council of Life Insurance
> Health Insurance Association of America
> 1850 K Street N.W.
> Washington, D.C. 20006

Figure out what you need to live on now. Not everyone gets a chance to make a new life plan and a new budget. It's like three or four New Years rolled into one, and it may take a few resolutions. Don't be surprised, though, when you fall short of perfection. There are three basic financial rules. Even upgrading them to allow for inflation, they still apply to everyone. Ready?

1. Figure your net income, that is, after income tax and deductions. If you have been among the increasing numbers of double-income families, this can be a sobering moment of truth. At least you have an income. For those widows who have never worked or who have been out of the work force from some fifteen to thirty years, the bottom line can look absolutely terrifying.

2. Figure on spending about half your income on shelter and food. The recommended percentages are 31 percent for housing costs (that's *costs,* including maintenance, not just rent or mortgage payments), and 23 percent for all food, including restaurant meals. A warning: the lower your in-

come, the more likely you are to exceed the one-half rule. You'll have to economize somewhere else.

3. Savings. Here's the rough one. Find a way to save— and tell me the secret. I have nothing to fall back on myself, except my native wit and my rather well-cushioned rear end. But you should aim (they say) for an amount in savings equal to 10 percent of your net income. When you have that, give a thought to your IRA. Then you can put something into other less inaccessible non-risk investments such as U.S. government treasury notes or certificates of deposit.

When the interest is high, you can't go wrong taking out a short-term certificate of deposit through your bank or your savings and loan association. The minimum amount of money required depends on the institution, as does the payment. The higher the amount, and the longer you arrange to leave it there, the higher interest you will receive. As for the government treasury notes, bills, and bonds, here's a brief rundown. The treasury bill, at a minimum of $10,000, rising at $1000 a shot over that, is bought at discount for less than a year. The amount you pay to purchase it depends on how close to the due date it is. You collect the full amount on maturity. The difference between the discount price you paid and the amount you receive when you cash in the bill is the "interest" you make on it. A treasury note can be purchased for from one to five years and pays interest semiannually. A treasury bond is purchased for over five years. There is a range of denominations and interest rates vary from year to year. Check with your bank of savings and loan association.

You can sell your treasury bill at any time. There is no fluctuation of value; the amount you receive depends on how long you have held it. If you sell a note or a bond, you will get less than its face value at maturity. It's better to hang on to it/them if you can.

The advantages of all the treasury stuff is that it is easily liquidated if you need instant cash for an emergency, and it's guaranteed by the government. The disadvantage is that it's a slim market. Beyond emergency funds, it's probably not too wise to go heavily into the interest-bearing things. By this time, though, you're getting into the stock market and that is beyond the scope of this book. I really am addressing women to whom the stock market will never be a consuming interest. Survival is uppermost in our minds.

The secret of savings, according to money expert Sylvia Porter, is to consider your savings an unavoidable expense and allow for it automatically. I'm not sure whether that's called discipline or forethought.

Now you can, if you're lucky, set up your income in accordance with your predicted outgo. Easier said than done. In these tough times, with the cost of living so uncomfortably high, few life insurance policies and pensions are going to provide all the income a widow needs. But there are some cushions, depending on your situation, and it might be wise to take stock of them right away. First of all, there is your husband's Social Security. It pays benefits for minor children (under the age of 19) directly to the widow. If the children go to college, they can continue to receive it directly for several more years. I don't want to be too specific, because a lot of these arrangements are subject to change. Social Security also pays a death payment (quite nominal) for burial costs. Widows' benefits do not begin until age 60 at the earliest. If you can afford to wait until you're 65, you'll be paid more. That can be a long five years for some, though.

To find out about your Social Security benefits, you pick up the phone and dial your local office listed under government Health and Human Services and report your husband's death. You can either go into the office then or if you are unable to do that, arrange for someone to call on you to help you make your claim. You will need: 1) your husband's death certificate, 2) his Social Security card, 3) your Social Security card, 4) your birth certificate, 5) your marriage certificate, and 6) your children's birth certificates, if they qualify for benefits. By the way, when you apply for the death certificate, ask for about ten copies. You will find you'll need them to make all your claims. You may know your husband is gone, but other people have to be convinced before they'll give you money.

It's like a scavenger hunt, gathering up these documents. Once you have them together, it's a good idea to keep them in a safe place, because you'd be amazed at how often you may have to refer to them, especially the death certificate and the Social Security card. If you leave the country, for example, your checks will follow you, but if there's ever a problem, the magic S.S. number is what's going to solve it. Veterans' Benefits may be another source of income to you, so be sure to contact your local Veterans' Association, if your husband was a veteran. There is a burial benefit, and there is also a pension benefit quite separate from the Social Security system. So keep on asking questions.

Then you have to check the terms of your husband's pension plan and find out what's coming to you. It's possible you may be dismayed and disappointed if you didn't do some planning and discussing before the fact. A number of choices can be made by a man on retirement, and if he thought he was going to live forever he may have opted for a pension plan that took little account of his widow. The more you and he had, the less you may have now. As for women, they have been ripped off for years by discriminatory pension plans, only just being repaired and improved. If you happen to read this book before your husband has died, do some checking now on the spousal payments of his pension plan, as well as on your own pension plan (if any). If it's too late, join the thousands of women (not only widows) who are making their grievances and needs concerning pension plans known.

What you're looking for, ultimately, are your options and your money. Your aim is to try to pay as little tax as possible on the lump sums you receive, because you need all the capital you can lay your hands on. But lump sums are too often taxable, and tax can be sizable, so do stop and think about the size and timing of the lump sum. Here's a dandy little rule I was told: if the money you are getting is taxable, ask what your options are. How are you going to learn anything if you don't ask questions? But try to ask someone who knows the answers.

Ask yourself a lot of questions, too. How much do you need? How long will it last? How much basic income can you count on each month? What other potential sources of income are there? Are the children old enough to work, or will they be soon? Should you take a course to increase your earning power? If you are already working, will your income plus your other sources be enough to tide you over? Or if you are a younger widow with children still at home, will you have to take your settlements in fairly big lumps over a short period of time to tide you over?

Tide you over to what? Tide you over to the point where you can bring in extra income of your own or to the point where you need less income because your children have left home—or both.

If you decide you have to work to supplement your income, and most widows do, perhaps you need some job-training before you can qualify to enter the work force or, if you already have a job, to increase your skills and hence your income. You may want to take your settlement in large monthly payments over a period of two (five? ten?) years until you are able to qualify and become a breadwinner yourself.

The first important thing is to establish your immediate needs. Talk them over with your life insurance agent and settle on the amount of money required. Even if it's not going to last very long at the rate you need it, at least it will give you time to plan. Spread the money out as far as it will go.

As your children leave the nest, expenses will decrease, but not that much, unless you move. A house costs almost the same to run whether there are four or three or only one person living in it. Taxes remain the same, and heating almost. You might use a little less water and electricity, but some costs are depressingly fixed.

In the meantime, there are lots of ways to economize. Everyone, according to a supermarket survey of buying habits, is buying more rice and pasta these days to supplement the meat. You can do that. Get a cookbook on Mexican or Italian or Chinese food from the library and start experimenting, if you haven't already, with more economical types of cooking. It's a North American myth that we need to eat all that expensive beef. We may be the last generation to believe it, too, because our grain-fed cattle are using grains the rest of the world's people could use to eat.

You can cut back on clothing, too, and social and recreational activities automatically get cut off once you are a widow. In fact, you'll save so much money in that department you'll have to have a party once in a while for the sake of your morale.

Magazines and newspapers are full of budget and cost-cutting ideas. Here are a few I picked up:

1. If you get a raise or a gift of money or any unlooked-for, unexpected income, pretend you didn't. Don't spend it. Put it into your savings account, or into a certificate of deposit instead, if it's big enough.

2. Get rid of your loose change. I save my dimes and quarters now for the laundry machines in my apartment. Nickels and pennies go into Matt's piggy bank—a painless way for him to save some money.

3. Don't carry credit cards with you. Or if you feel you must, try leaving them at home one week a month. See if you don't spend less money. Money experts say people spend at least 10 percent more when they buy by credit card. Be sure and keep a com-

plete record of your credit cards so that you can report them instantly if they are lost or stolen. The easiest way is to spread them out on a piece of paper and Xerox them all at your local post office.

4. If you have a bank loan or a system of payments on a car or furniture, don't stop making the payments after you've paid up. Just put the same amount regularly into your savings account. It's called discipline. Incidentally, when you take out a bank loan, find out if it is insured. The debt is automatically paid off then in the event of your death. Ask!

5. Don't carry as much cash as you did, if you did. See how little you can get along on. (But don't be chintzy.)

6. Shop for groceries right after a meal so that you're not hungry and reaching impulsively for food. Impulses in supermarkets can add 25 percent to your grocery bill. Make a shopping list and stick to it.

7. That means making a menu plan for the week. A plan saves not only money but time. I always make my menu plan with the fridge door open, checking the contents to see what has to be used up. I've written a cookbook about using up leftovers *(Encore: The Leftovers Cookbook)* and I maintain you can pay for the book in the first two weeks of using it. After that, what you save is gravy—always good for leftovers.

8. Use the coupons you are constantly being bombarded with, but use them wisely. Don't buy something you don't use and if you buy something to send away for a refund, be sure to follow through.

9. Try saying no for a week. No chocolate bars, no magazines, no movies, no wine, no meeting a friend for lunch or coffee. You might even lose some weight, and I have met very few women who ever minded that.

10. Walk instead of taking the car, or take public transit. You'll not only save money; you'll get some much-needed exercise.

If you have a car and continue to drive it, you should let your car insurance agent know that your husband is dead, and make sure you are covered for driving as the principal driver. This caution does not apply to women who don't drive or who don't own a car. For those who don't drive it is a question of selling the car or giving it to one of the children. Or taking driving lessons. What I needed was geography lessons.

I had a different kind of decision to make. Just weeks before his death, my husband had ordered a new car, a big heavy one equipped with all the extras: stereo, 8-track tape deck, cruise control, etc. It was a floating living room, hardly the kind of vehicle a lorn widow lady needed. So one of the first things I had to do was to go down to the car dealer and make arrangements for a smaller, more modest car to suit my reduced needs.

If you're having trouble with your car, start asking more questions. There are places you can go to do your own car repairs where you just pay for the parts, but I'm sure not many of us want to go that far. Even allowing for my liberated conscience, I also have to allow for my personal preference and ineptitude. I prefer to have someone do the work for me. I was very proud of myself the first time I filled the gas tank at a self-serve gas station—that's as far as I want to go with do-it-yourself car maintenance. If you feel the same way, find yourself a reputable car dealer or mechanic and stay with him. Ask around. People have favorites. You're bound to find someone who will make the car sing for you without charging the earth. Bear in mind that earth costs more these days. So does gasoline.

It's a good idea to join an automobile club. There is a nominal fee and you'll feel absolutely smug the first time you get free towing from some unlikely spot where the car refused to start, or got stuck, or stubborn, as cars do.

The price of gasoline is going to continue to rise; we all know that. If you live in a city with good public transportation, you may find that you will save a lot of money by getting rid of the car entirely. On the other hand, suburbia and young children make a car more of a necessity. It has been proven several times by people with heads for figures that taking taxis can be cheaper than owning and driving a car in a city now, but it's inconvenient when it rains. Older widows I know take taxis, but a lot of them take other people, too—out of their way. People drive widows and save them the taxi fares. You have to figure your options, and not only on insurance.

If you decide to buy a car, however, that's a whole new experience. That first car I bought after my husband died, that wasn't buying a car, that was just writing a check; he had already arranged the money for that floating living room. But four years later, I actually bought a car of my own. I shopped; I asked questions; I checked *Consumers' Report;* and I got my very first bank loan. That was the most important thing of all. I now exist in the world of finance. I have a credit rating.

There is a gray area surrounding women and credit. As a widow you are more respectable than a divorcée in the eyes of the cliché-ridden public, and you can often coast on your husband's credit rating if you don't have one yourself. Lots of widows simply don't tell the various department stores and oil companies that their husbands are deceased and go on paying their bills. Few companies notice that Mr.'s signature no longer appears on the checks. Some of the big ones don't care, it seems; widows I know who have gone to the trouble of informing them of change of name and status at the time of a move have simply had cards reissued with the address changed and nothing more.

Until you have borrowed money in your name and paid it back, you don't have a credit rating. Even if you don't need money right now, it might be a good idea to go through all the motions; at least, it used to be a good idea. Now, with interest rates what they are, you have to weigh what you're doing more carefully. If you invested the money, the interest rate would probably exceed your interest income, and that's a bind. Although there are no discriminatory laws on the books regarding women and credit, and although company and bank policies now are stated to be favorably inclined to dealing with women, there is still a gap between theory and practice. It takes a while for company policy to seep down into the ranks of the clerks and managers who will be dealing with you. Horror stories abound: about the working mother, a widow, sole support of her family, with a good income, who was required to get the signature of her sixteen-year-old son before she could get a department store credit card; about another single woman who had managed to keep her family and herself for years but who couldn't get a mortgage without her father's signature—and he was seventy-five and living on his Social Security! My widowed mother was issued a charge card with Mr. on it. She sent it back explaining she was Mrs. They sent her a new card with her correct title but a lower credit rating. The *s* meant $ to the bank. My bank has no category for widow in its application form for a special service account. A widowed friend of mine met confusion in the form she had to fill out when she wanted to open a high-interest, no-checking savings account at her bank. "If widowed or divorced," read the form, "give husband's name and address." Yes indeed.

That widow has this advice to give: don't be timid. Bear down. If you're asking for a loan, walk in with a list of your assets, both fixed and liquid, and "shove it at them." You almost have to convince them you don't need the loan in order to get it! Don't try to reform the system. If they balk at you, say you'll go elsewhere or ask for a higher authority. If that sounds like assertiveness training, you're absolutely right.

If you get or already have credit cards, use them, by all means. But use them as if you were using cash. It's safer that way. I have found that it is better to operate on a cash basis. Widows and freelance writers (and I am both) have this in common: their futures are more precarious than most and their incomes are smaller, not to say variable. So I do not buy on time. I stay out of debt beyond my current monthly expenses. I would resent paying the 27 to 33 percent interest if I merely paid my minimum monthly payment on a credit card. I can't afford that, and neither can you. Debt is a downward spiral that widows should stay out of. If you do fall hopelessly behind and owe everyone and the milkman, then take a bank loan and pay off everything at once. The banks charge lower interest rates than the credit card companies, and you preserve your image as a responsible, bill-paying, adult human being.

One of the biggest debts I had was the mortgage on the house, but this was wiped out by a life insurance policy. There are policies for mortgage cancellation. Find out if you have one. Even if you do not have such a policy, it might be wise, if there is enough money, to pay off the mortgage and own your home clear. But it depends, of course, on the interest rates. If your mortgage has a very low interest charge riding on it, you'd be crazy to clean it up with today's high-costing money. Every case, as always, is individual. Ask questions before you do anything you'll be sorry for.

Still, it's a good feeling to own your own home clear. Little widow ladies tend to feel more secure if they are women of property, and real estate continues to be one of the best investments you can make.

Here is another little-known fact I was told. Normally, mortgage companies want an interest bonus when the mortgage is paid off. But if a widow explains that she is using a life insurance policy to pay off the mortgage, the bonus may be waived. (Mine was.) The moral to the story is: it doesn't hurt to ask! Write a personal letter. Big institutions are human, too, often more human than an individual who holds only one or two mortgages and needs his income from the interest.

But while we're on the subject of your home, you will be deciding sooner or later whether or not you're going to stay there. Make it later. One of the most important things a widow can learn is to sit tight, and this applies to sex as well as to money. Make few quick decisions, at least, few basic ones. You will have enough to do getting your heart and head together. Don't do anything rash. Wait at least a year, if you possibly can, before you decide whether to move or to make any other changes in your life. Your children will appreciate this, too, if you still have children at home. Life will have changed enough for all of you without imposing other upheavals. So get your money settled, try to establish a living plan for the immediate future, but *don't do anything drastic!*

The future stretches a long way ahead of us. Widows with younger children must pay attention to their needs and the more immediate future, but all of us have to prepare for a long, lonely road with whatever resources we have, and sometimes they are extremely limited.

You wonder as you grow older whether you will outlive your money. Good question, and I have no easy answer to that. Most older widows I know are much more fearful of living than of dying. The fact is that the majority of the nation's poor are women, single women, for whatever reason single. As one woman put it, most women are "one man away from welfare."

Fixed incomes become less and less effective as prices keep rising with no end in sight. You simply have to try to salt something away for that twilight zone we are all approaching while seeking the best returns for your money right now. "God will provide," goes the proverb, "and I wish He would till He does."

"From birth to eighteen," said Sophie Tucker, "a girl needs good parents. From eighteen to thirty-five she needs good looks. From thirty-five to fifty-five she needs a good personality. From fifty-five on, she needs good cash." The average age at which a woman is widowed is fifty-six, and what she needs is good cash. And no matter what the amount, you are the one who has to make the decisions about your widow's mite. It's your future you're talking about, and there ain't nobody else going to look after you.

There are some wives today who still scarcely know how to write a check. I could do that, but I couldn't balance a checkbook. I still can't, because I can't add or subtract worth a damn. But I can stay within a budget and I pay my bills on time and I'm juggling a job and feeding my family and I feel stronger than I have ever felt.

It's not easy and it's not simple, but there are helps and guides and signposts along the way, and if you don't know where you're going, consult a map, that is, an expert. *Sylvia Porter's New Money Book for the 80's*, for example, will tell you all about every aspect of spending and saving, with explanations and practical advice.

Too many husbands, and their lawyers, have been telling too many women for too long not to "worry their pretty little heads about that"—that being money. When the pretty head is widowed, it gets a headache from not knowing. Many widows lose financially by not understanding the language of the lawyer and the accountant, or else they lose friends, as I lost my friend the insurance agent.

Here's one other simple piece of advice someone told me. "Never, never sign anything without reading every word and understanding it."

You need all the support and knowledge you can get. Check the resources of your local library and the courses available in your area. When you've gone as far as reading and study can take you, don't be afraid to ask more questions. It's amazing how much information you can get if you ask a direct question!

Somewhere along the way, you're going to realize that there's more to this business of survival than mere money. You'll start asking just how much you really need, and then you'll start asking as never before what is really important to you. You may be surprised.

A few years ago now, curious about what it would be like to live on the Old Age Pension—your Social Security—I left my apartment in Toronto and went to live in a rooming house for a few weeks, in clothes borrowed from the donations room of a women's hostel, with an extra blanket and my soup pot, with no other resources but the amount of money that a woman over the age of sixty-five would receive from the government. It was a revelation. I learned a lot about myself as well as about money. I wanted to meet my old lady in the future, that is, me, waiting down the road apiece. She prays, too, and counts her blessings.

I hope you will be able to do the same.

❋ 5
Moving on

> *How quickly, in one instant, years of happy life be-*
> *come only memories!*
>
> PEARL BUCK

There is a phrase engineers use to describe the position of an object when it stops moving. It is called the "angle of repose." Your husband has reached his angle of repose, but you haven't. You haven't stopped moving yet. As long as we live we keep on changing.

The first autumn after Bill died, I went ahead as usual and made jams, jellies, pickles, etc. I don't have a second hand on my watch or my kitchen clock. I always used to use my husband to time my jelly-stirring (or count "a-thousand-and-one-''). So when I had to stir my jelly that first fall, I ran upstairs and got his watch to help me out. It was the first time I had looked at it. The date had changed—it had stopped twelve hours after he died.

I can stand that, I thought. I can stand that. And I can. I can stand anything. I didn't know that before. You can, too.

I haven't made jelly since, or pickles, but for other reasons than you might suspect. First, my family did not use up the supplies within the year as they did before. Second, I lost my interest in cooking. Third, I became too busy doing other things. Fourth, there is no storage space in my new home for preserves. You see, I moved.

Divorce, quipped a recent divorcée, is learning how to change your own lightbulbs. That applies to widowhood, too. I know there are lots of married women who change the lightbulbs, and take out the garbage, too, but it is a comforting knowledge that there is another, usually taller, person in the house who can change a ceiling bulb or get something down from the top shelf in the kitchen without standing on a stepstool.

There are men who are not handy around the house: my father wasn't; my husband was only slightly better; my son John is a whiz. One out of three isn't bad. It's a stereotype that says men have to be good at fixing toaster plugs and unstopping clogged toilets while women sew on the buttons and make the porridge. If I lose a button I might as well throw the garment away. I'm three years behind in my mending.

But when one becomes a widow, suddenly the home chores become terribly important. Who's going to do them? Who's going to applaud you when you do them? It's not only that it's work you have to do yourself; it's also that there's no zest in doing it. Why bother? Do you want to put up Christmas lights this year? Do you need to put bedding plants in? Does the fence really need painting?

A lot of the inertia of grief spills over into the process of living. C. S. Lewis commented on it in his book *A Grief Observed:* "No one," he wrote, "ever told me about the laziness of grief. Except at my job—where the machine seems to run on much as usual—I loathe the slightest effort. . . . It's easy to see why the lonely become untidy."

It's not only the grass-mowing, the snow-shoveling, the broken windows, garbage, leaky faucets and eaves troughs, sticking doors, and burnt-out lightbulbs. Even more oppressive in the single-handed care and upkeep of a home are the major repairs and maintenance. It's making a decision, getting the thing done, and paying the bill—all for something you don't really care about as much anymore. Like every other problem widows face, it looms large because you're facing it alone. And there's no satisfaction in it when you do tackle a job, because who notices? Who cares?

If you think I'm giving you an argument for not owning a house, you're not completely right. Certainly I am not advising you to rush away from it. Running a house by yourself is only one more of the many challenges you face as a single person. It can be done. And there are rewards.

I have said elsewhere that you should not make any major decision—and moving would be a major one—hastily. Sit tight for at least a year, if you can, after your husband's death, while you take stock and measure your own abilities and attitudes. But don't let the house go to seed while you sit there. In the same way, you have been urged by your friends (haven't you?) not to "let yourself go," you mustn't neglect the maintenance of your home. Your house is probably your biggest single investment. Don't be afraid to spend some money on it. Take care of it. Then when you do decide to move, you'll get your money out of it.

In these heady days of the feminist movement, there are wonderful changes taking place which may make your tasks easier. There are courses springing up all over the country for women to learn how to carpenter, do electrical repairs, car maintenance, upholstery, etc., and women are taking them and learning how to cope, to their great satisfaction. I know a single woman who does all her own remodeling. If there is something she doesn't know how to do, she takes a course on the subject and learns. Her home is a showcase, an apartment in a beautiful old house, and she has done all the refinishing, carpentry, papering, painting, and electrical installations herself. A former neighbor of mine, married, took a woodworking course and built a magnificent pool table for her husband and sons. It is a work of art. The only things she bought ready-made were the balls and the cues. Now she's paneling the rec room. And there are women to whom gardening is no chore, as it is to me, who find great satisfaction in keeping their gardens glowing and beautiful. And then there are others like me who would rather have everything done for them. I'll stand by the sidelines and cheer and provide sandwiches and coffee and first aid, if necessary, for the workers. I was fortunate that my son John was handy around the house. At fourteen he took over the house, pool, and yard maintenance and I never had cause for complaint. But I realized that first summer when he went away to camp how dependent I was on him. I couldn't have done it by myself, nor did I want to.

One of the clichés of widowhood is the clingy little neighborhood widow who needs help from her neighbors' husbands. There were times, I'll admit, when I found that help necessary. I tried to avoid criticism by inviting both husband and wife over for drinks or coffee and a snack while I explained my problem. That way I got some company and some free help, and the wife was assured that I had no designs on her husband outside of his plumbing or financial skills or whatever. There really are problems you encounter that only men can solve, but you do have to be careful how you go about asking them to solve them. Their wives resent it, and men often get the idea that that isn't the only problem you have that needs a man's touch.

But that's something else again. The point I am trying to make is that, ept or not, it is possible for you to go on living where you have been living and to cope by yourself. The libraries are full of how-to books, and some of them are written especially for women.

Staying on in the last home you and your husband shared together has its own kind of comfort. The pictures on the walls were probably discussed and hung by both of you in consultation; all the decorating decisions surrounding you were probably joint ones. A presence lingers that is sustaining. On the other hand, when and if the time comes to move, that can be good, too. As one widow said, "Moving is like closing the wound; you're healed and you move on." Take your time, though. Think about it. No rush.

I'm afraid we rushed my mother when my father died. I didn't know as much then as I do now. We thought the reasons were good and valid, but I can see now she should have had more time. Moving is a traumatic experience and should not follow too hard on the heels of the death of one's mate. The house still retains echoes and memories which are comforting. Your mind resists change. Any decision you make is apt to be woolly-headed and unreasonable. And the inertia of the body makes one incapable of the large amounts of energy required for moving.

On the other hand, it often happens now that a woman can be stranded by the death of her husband in a city that is strange to her. I myself had lived in Stratford only five years when Bill died. The friends we had made were obviously not lifelong friends. That can make a big difference in terms of long-term support and concern. If you find yourself in a strange community, perhaps in spite of my admonitions not to move too quickly or hastily, the best thing would be to move back to your hometown. I know two widows who did just that, both within a month of their husband's death, and it was the right thing for them to do. Both of them have since remarried, by the way. I don't know if there's a moral to that story or not.

My reasons for moving were as complex as yours might be. I was tired of taking care of the house all by myself. I was tired of living in a small city, one which I discovered did not adapt easily to singles in its midst. I was tired of living in a ghetto of women and, particularly, of widows. I felt things would be different in a larger city, and they have been. But most of all, I was tired of driving on Highway 401 to Toronto. I like driving, but not in blizzards or sleet or ice storms. And on the highway as nowhere else I was aware of the responsibility I had to take very good care of my children's only parent.

"Drive carefully," John would say as I left the house. "I don't want to live with someone else."

I was spending too much time on the highway, because all my work was in Toronto. I knew I could increase my income if I moved, because I would be where the work was. Driving time is unproductive time. Incidentally, a move for financial reasons such as mine is deductible.

I didn't know many widows my age, but the ones I did know were affected by my decision. One of them also sold her house and moved out of town, as I did. Another put her house on the market, quit her job, took a course, and found a better job. Another stayed where she was but made envious noises and became more dissatisfied with her life. She needs another catalyst.

For many different reasons, a widow may find that the home she maintained when she was her husband's wife no longer suits her needs. It may be too expensive, too much trouble to keep up, too large as the family keeps shrinking, too empty when the widow is left alone. If enough time has passed that the reasons for moving are based on common sense and logic and not on some emotional gut reaction, then by all means move.

A move for a widow usually means a reduction in space. Whether you move from one house or apartment to another, or from a house to an apartment, the new space is usually smaller than the old space—that's part of the reason for moving, isn't it? That means getting rid of a lot of the stuff in the present space in order to fit into the new, smaller space. It means, finally, taking stock of your past, your marriage, and your possessions. And it means finding out more things about yourself. Such as, how important are possessions to you? How important is space? How much space? A garden? Neighbors? Memories? Habits?

Take your time. Consider it the biggest spring (or fall) cleaning you've ever undertaken. Go over everything. Find out what your children want, and give it to them or save it for them. Have a garage sale. Sell things or give them away, but get rid of them.

Strange reactions happen, but welcome them. This is another purge and it's valuable. I found I was reliving a future that was no longer going to occur. Things I had put away for our old age together I no longer needed, so they went out. My scenario is different; I need different props. It was not only my past I was clearing; it was also my future, and that's valuable, if somewhat painful.

We end up owning many things not by choice but by accident, because we needed something in a hurry, because someone else thought we needed something and gave it to us, because it was on sale, because it fit a room or a specific purpose at the time. How seldom it is given to anyone to choose again, or if not to choose, at least to discriminate! What you finally end up with, when you move as a widow, is what you choose to keep. Finally, and perhaps for the first time in your life, and maybe only in a negative way, your possessions make a statement about *you*.

We live in such a materialistic age; we all accumulate things like squirrels. I can't tell you what a pleasure it was to begin to divest myself of some of my possessions. I felt like Diogenes with his bowl. Remember the story of the Greek philosopher who owned nothing but a bowl in which he collected the food he begged to keep himself alive? One day he tripped and broke his bowl and he said, "At last! I'm free!" I still own too much, but I own a lot less than I did. It's nice to be lighter and freer than I was.

I had the biggest garage sale in the world, and that was a revelation in itself. I heartily recommend garage sales. People will buy anything if it's on sale, and I mean anything. There is a little paperback with complete advice on such sales, and most women's magazines have tips on them every spring. All you have to do is go to one or two and learn how for yourself. I sold tired Christmas wrap and decorations and lights, broken hockey sticks, boxes of torn sheets, threadbare towels and rags (useful for painters and mechanics, I found), toys and clothes and ornaments and glasses, old dolls with the eyes blunk out, tablecloths and placemats and utensils, clothes, appliances, furniture, carpets and lawn chairs, and my neighbor's new broom that she swept my garage floor with and left leaning against a wall. I sold my past and parts of my future that no longer existed. I'm afraid I sold some of my children's past and future, too, and I feel sorry about that.

Storage in my parents' home remained available to me until long after I was married. I didn't fully claim all my possessions until we were living in our third home. I'm sorry I couldn't grant that kind of carefree space to my children. But Liz is less of a packrat than I am, perhaps because I am one. And there's still a box of Barbie doll stuff in my apartment locker belonging to Kate.

Moving is harder on the children who are at home. I had hoped to spare them the move at least until John was finished high school, but as I became more and more busy in Toronto and unhappy in Stratford, I realized that two years out of my life at my age were more important than two years out of his life at his age, so I didn't wait. It is hard on kids to move in their teens, late in their high school years. They have no time to form new allegiances. They become aliens when it is desperately important for them to belong. I know that, and I'm sorry, and it's something you should consider if it applies. But John found a compensation in the fact that I was nicer to live with and around a lot more (instead of on the highway) once we'd moved. There are times you have to make the decision for yourself and let the others fall into line with you.

It's a case of weighing the advantages and disadvantages. There are times when you have to cut your losses and run. You do it materially when you move. You have to take a beating on some of the things you're selling off, as you might expect. You can't get much for second-hand furniture. You'll just have to consider the difference between what you paid originally and what you finally received for it as rent for the use of it. You can't take it with you—there's no room. So move on without it.

And that's what you have to do emotionally, too. You can't sit down and wither in the past. You can't wait out a future that doesn't exist. Take your memories with you, by all means, but move on.

❀6
The working widow

Those who do not complain are never pitied.

JANE AUSTEN

There are ten and a half million widowed women in the United States today. Just under a third of them lose their husbands before they themselves reach the age of forty. The median income of widows is $5,052. You may well have to work (if you're lucky) in order to survive.

Widows have a relatively low participation in the work force, because many of them are older and of retirement age. Yet the median income of women over the age of sixty-five is $4,226—it's nothing to look forward to. With fixed incomes and inadequate pensions balancing more and more poorly against ever-increasing inflation, even older widows find themselves attempting to increase their incomes through full- or part-time work.

According to *Widows Study,* a 1971 never-repeated report by the Life Underwriters' Training Council and Life Insurance Marketing and Research Association, the incomes of widows' families go down an average of 44 percent from pre-death levels. The difference in income, before and after, is, as might be expected, in direct proportion to the size of the husband's income. There was actually an increase of 4 percent when the family income had been less than $3,000 but also a sickening decrease of 57 percent when the family income had been $15,000 or more. It's not surprising, in light of today's ever-increasing cost of living, to learn that almost six in ten (58 percent) of the widows had incomes that fell below the amount required to maintain their former living standards.

Nothing has changed since then. If anything, conditions are worse. According to Barbara Ehrenreich and Karin Stallard in a Special Report in *Ms.* magazine in July/August, 1982, women are the "nouveau poor." Even if it hasn't happened yet, widowhood may take away your membership in the middle class. It's called the feminization of poverty.

And so—a lot of widows have to go to work. Trained or not, if a widow needs more money than she has coming in, she must find a means of supplementing her income. The question is what will she do? There are as many answers to that as there are people, and both are a constant source of surprise. I know one widow who has indulged a lifelong love of dolls by starting a dolls' hospital. Her painstaking, loving work is much in demand. Another widow was instrumental in starting a widows' counseling service through a local Y; she went to a community college to take the necessary courses and is now helping to run the service on a continuing, paid basis. My mother-in-law in her day took in a boarder to make ends meet. Half my babysitters when my children were small were older widows who turned their experience with children and their abiding interest in people into a service that is always in demand. What a widow does depends on her training, her age, her children, and her opportunities. Fortunately, at least partly because of the feminist movement, there are more opportunities than ever. Doors are opening.

But they don't open all by themselves. Neither do they present themselves as easy solutions. Remember the short story "The Lady or the Tiger," in which the hero had to choose between two identical doors and thereby seal his fate? Well, your problem is similar when you end up at forty-plus trying to decide what to do with the rest of your life.

But you are no longer alone in this search. With the increasing divorce rate, and the number of housewives who are returning to the labor force after, or whether or not, their children are grown, there are many women like you who need to assess and upgrade their skills and find a new career. Ehrenreich and Stallard are bleak about it: "Whether through divorce, desertion, or death, an estimated 85 percent of American women can expect to have to support themselves (if not themselves and their children) at some time in their lives."

It's not going to be easy. The economic climate keeps getting harsher, and what cushions and help there used to be have been cut and trimmed and eliminated. Upgrading educational and employment programs are either not as plentiful as they were or have been drastically reduced. The traditional jobs that remain open to women are among the lowest paying on the wage scale, and it's still a fact that women receive only 59 percent of what men are paid.

Women tend to go into six or seven different occupations outside the home: waitressing, clerking, selling, teaching, nursing, and so on. Although teaching and nursing pay a little better, with the cutbacks in school and hospital budgets these jobs are almost impossible to get now. I tried to get a teaching job when my husband died, but the places were filled. The only regular job open was as women's editor of my local weekly newspaper, and that paid so little that my lawyer suggested that I try to free-lance. I had always been a writer, but I had never had to make a living at it. There's a difference. Anyway, it worked. So did I. Now I am inclined to believe that women must try to create their own jobs.

In any case, you will have to investigate your options very carefully. Start by taking a good look at yourself, even before you look at the job or the new training you may need. What are your attitudes? Your likes and dislikes? If you can't stand talking to strangers, don't get a job as a receptionist. If you get lonely without people, don't hide yourself in the stacks of a library. If you think men make better electricians than women, think again. When typewriters were invented, it was said that women could never learn to handle such a machine, because it required more dexterity than a woman could ever achieve!

Even if you had a specific skill or training, you may need brushing-up—a refresher course in bookkeeping or shorthand, some practice to get your speed back at that masculine typewriter, and a word-processing course wouldn't hurt. Some fields have changed so much that your refresher course might well take one or two years back at school.

I know one woman who found so many changes in her field (biology) that she was really dismayed, because her memory wasn't what it used to be. So she took a course in memory training first. But she kept forgetting to go to the classes. That's a joke. Sort of.

Some of the new women's magazines dedicated to the working woman have ideas and suggestions for job retraining and job creation as well as moonlighting—not a bad idea if you have young children at home. Home jobs are gaining in popularity, too, but the danger of child labor abuse has already been recognized. I work at home, and no one has ever been able to do it for me. The same might not be true for someone who does piecework on her own sewing machine. Exploitation is just around the corner, and not just for the child.

If further training is necessary before a suitable job can be found, there are more resources available now than there ever have been. If a woman already holds a college degree, she can take further courses at most colleges across the country. Information and catalogues are available, as well as guides and suggestions for grants and scholarships. Some colleges now allow credits for "life experience" to mature students—people past "a certain age" who register as students. There is no uniformity about this benefit. Ask about it when you write for catalogues and other information. Inquire, too, about bursaries, scholarships, and student loan plans.

Then there are all the community colleges that have sprung up across the country. They offer one- and two-year courses in a vast range of subjects, usually directly applicable to jobs. Most of the colleges have some sort of women's guidance centers, designed to help women in their training.

All right, you've done your personal inventory. You are trained and ready and you know what you want to do. Now you can take a look at the job. You have to consider the built-in costs. If child-care is necessary, that is a major expense. Consider day-care centers. The lack of adequate facilities to care for the children of working mothers has been one of the prongs of the feminist movement. There still is a dreadful gap between need and supply. Somehow, the needs of young children have to be met while the single mother is out earning the family bread. Often, in the case of a preschool child, a relative or close friend or neighbor is the answer—but make it a financial arrangement if you can. It lasts longer.

There is also a difficult twilight zone in children's ages that presents a different problem and requires a different solution. What about the children who are of school age, fairly competent, but still too young to make their own lunch or not quite responsible enough to be at loose ends after school until someone comes home? School lunches, or again a reliable neighbor (on a paid basis to guarantee continuity), and after-school programs are all necessities in this case.

My youngest son was signed up term after term for after-school programs, for which I was deeply grateful. What was more, the school allowed single parents and working mothers to sign up first, showing great understanding of our pressures. Matthew ended up knowing more about macramé, cooking, ceramics, creative dance, floor hockey, and woodworking than he cared to, but I knew he was constructively occupied until I got home.

There are other, personal expenses. Are you going to have to spend more on clothes to look presentable for this job? If you can't wear pantsuits at least part of the time you're going to be spending more on pantyhose. (Doesn't everyone use up her runned ones under pantsuits?) How far do you have to travel to get to the job? Can you afford the transportation costs? And the time it takes you to get to and from your work? Your lifestyle changes again when you take a full-time job; make sure it is a change for the better, one that you will welcome for the challenge and stimulus and not one that is going to drag you down and make you tired and more discouraged than ever.

If you take a full-time job, chances are you will have some sort of company or group policy, and chances are equally good that there is a disability clause in it. Check it out. It could be worse, at this stage of your life, if you were disabled and unable to work than if you were dead, for all practical purposes. Child support continues to be necessary no matter where you are—in a wheelchair or in a bed—so be sure to find out about this.

Disability, I have discovered, really is a fate worse than death, and a fate far more feared by women. With good reason. Odds are, for women of almost any age, that they are more likely to suffer disability than death. Self-employed, with no access to group insurance plans with disability clauses, I have always been consciously aware that I am my children's only parent, when setting out to drive somewhere. I have an automatic insurance program on every flight I take, and it comforts me.

I have no fear of death. After I lost my death wish and had reconciled myself to sticking around until I was allowed to leave, I still found that life was not that sweet nor death that fearsome. I used to do a spot check on myself, a swift emotional pulse-taking every time I took off in a plane (along with the prayer I offer to give it an extra lift). I found that I looked up, rather than down, and I was always ready to leave. Mostly, I gave thought to my children, especially Matthew, my youngest, who has always needed extra help. About a year ago, he was with me on a trip—a pilgrimage, really, to meet his father's relatives in Scotland and England. We encountered severe turbulence for the first couple of hours of the flight, and when I did my spot check I found that all systems were go, because Matthew was with me.

"It's okay," I said to him. "We can crash, because we're together."

He didn't see it that way at all, I'm happy to say. With all the troubles he's had in his life, he thinks life is worth living, and it is. God has a purpose for him as He has for all of us.

If you're working full-time, you should investigate your company's pension plan. Certainly, women have been ripped off by pension plans in the past, but they're gradually improving. Most companies now include a pension or profit-sharing plan for their employees. You are not liable for income taxes on the money that your company sets aside annually for investment in your retirement plan, or on the interest or other earnings on the money while it stays in the plan. Uncle Sam holds off until you start to collect your benefits, and by that time, presumably, your tax blow will ease, because your income bracket will be lower when you quit working. A Qualified Savings Plan with your company is quite nice, because the company matches every dollar you put in with two dollars. What's more, it's portable; that is, you can take it with you if you change jobs and leave. There are some rules and restrictions about how long you have to be with the company before you qualify, however.

As a self-employed person I could have my own Keogh Plan for up to 15 percent of my income, with a ceiling of $200,000 (I'm in no danger of bumping my head!). It works like an IRA (see below); that is, it's a savings plan with interest. Like the corporate retirement plan or an IRA, both contributions and earnings from a Keogh plan are not taxable until they are withdrawn.

If you haven't already, and if you can, it's wise to set yourself up with an Individual Retirement Account. You can put in up to $2000 of your earned income per year, and this amount is deductible from your income tax. You can keep on paying into an IRA until you're seventy—presuming you're still earning—but you can't take any out without a penalty until you're fifty-nine. Again, by the time you take it out, presumably your other income will have decreased and you will not have to pay such a large tax on it.

It is likely, once you start working, that you will continue to do so until retirement age. This is your new vocation, beyond that of wife and mother. Take a look at your long-term goals and be sure you're going where you want to go. If you don't have any goals, maybe you should think about that, too. You're alone now. You're you. Who are you? And where are you going? What do you want? If you think I'm asking tough questions, you're right. I've been asking myself the same ones.

You have to keep on treating life as an adventure. Someone just pushed you out on a highwire and there's no safety net. Don't look down! Look ahead, and dazzle us all with your footwork. There may be fears that interfere with a successful new career. Fear of rejection. Fear of inability. Fear of competition. Fear of incompetence. Well, I'm not telling you to be unrealistic. No one expects you to *fly* off that highwire. But there's no sense being defeatist either. Don't panic. One step at a time, taken confidently, is going to get you to the other side.

Your maturity is one of your assets. No prospective employer is going to consider you a flighty young thing who's going to drop everything as soon as she finds a man, or worry about your leaving because you're pregnant (heaven forbid!). You can offer your own stability and resolution to succeed as definite pluses. Your very need is reassuring, because it means you won't be leaving in a hurry. And some of the special emotion reserved for widows also works for you. One widow told me she felt sorry for divorcées, because they were regarded as flighty; a widow with a child, on the other hand, like my friend, was pitied and revered and helped along the way.

Remember that employers are always looking for reliable, dependable employees with the appropriate skills to fill their vacancies.

Age isn't the problem that it was (though there is still a double standard), and there are, as noted, programs designed to help the woman over forty with job training and placement. However, an older woman may not be able to develop a marketable skill or she may find that she lacks the energy to work full-time. Some of the temporary help firms may be able to place her. Or consider this:

I have mentioned babysitters already, and sitting is a friendly, human way to earn extra money. But housekeeping is even more so. Every woman who has run a home of her own has a skill that she can consider selling. Unfortunately in North America today, people tend to look down on housekeepers or maids as "hired help." But they are worth their weight in gold and in very short supply. If you are alone, or have very few ties, you might consider taking on an adopted family. The pay is good, the expenses are nil, and there's built-in company. You'll actually work less than you did as mistress of your own household—there are rules about slave labor which, of course, don't apply to wives. Think about it.

For those women past retirement age who want to keep busy, paid or not, because time hangs heavy on their hands, volunteer jobs have become more and more interesting and challenging. Volunteers are much in demand and are always welcome.

If you lack the energy to do volunteer work on a regular basis but would still love to do something if only to keep up with other human beings, there are still things you can do.

Perhaps you have a skill that is of use to someone. When I was first married, the dean of women at my college asked me if I would help some newly arrived Chinese students who were having trouble with idiomatic English. My husband was taking a night course, so my students came to me on the night he was out, and we launched on their indoctrination. I did it for nothing, that is, no money, but I gained a great deal from it. I made new friends. You could do that. If you were a teacher, or even if you weren't, you could discuss the vagaries of our silly language with some young new Canadians or Americans, and you might even offer them some comforting advice about survival while you're at it.

The old golden rule still applies. When you're feeling rotten yourself, try to reach out to help someone else who feels rotten. You'll feel better making them feel better. There are still things you can do for other people which will make you feel valuable and useful. There are a lot of shut-ins right now, right across the country, and some of them are on accessible lists. The Meals on Wheels organizations have such lists; nursing homes have waiting lists; government welfare organizations have lists. Ask if you can volunteer to phone a few people, keep in touch with them, check on their health, chat and gossip and spend the time of day with them—by telephone. You can still talk, can't you? Reach out with your electronic tongue and help someone else. It's perfectly possible to make a good friend by voice alone. For that matter, it's possible to turn your friendly tongue into a paying proposition. There used to be a service in Toronto known as Tele-Check, which provided a daily phone call to a shut-in five days or seven days a week. In the case of no answer, the Tele-Check person then made a further appropriate phone call, either to the manager or superintendent of the building in which the shut-in lived, or to a neighbor, friend, or relative. Now this service is duplicated by an electronic device, they tell me. It's not the same as a human being. Life consists of more than breathing; and it's nice to spend your breath on conversation once in a while. You might consider starting this kind of human service in your town or city and earn a little money yourself without leaving home. You charge so much per phone call, or a flat rate per week. It's wise, though, to make the arrangements with a relative of the shut-in. Some people don't appreciate paid friendship, and I can't say that I blame them. No one ever said old age was easy.

There are several helpful hints I can pass on to a working widow which, like everything else in these scattered pages, I found out the hard way. The first is that you're going to get tired, tired as you have never been. There are times when it will seem that there is no respite. You will have gone the second mile and still there is no haven in sight. Well, weariness is like pain in many respects: you have to give in to it. Ride with it. Don't be ashamed to crawl into bed after dinner. Sometimes an hour is all you need. Sometimes it pays to go to bed early and stay there until morning.

There are so many times when you have to keep on working, running as you do from the job, the paying one, to another, the cooking and bottle-washing one, that it would be wise to recognize the times when you can afford to goof off. Who says the sheets have to be changed every Saturday, or whenever you used to change them? All the rules laid down in domestic science books and the women's magazines were written for someone else, someone with more time, more leisure, more devotion to good housekeeping than you now have—and more money. So what if the place doesn't get dusted as often? No one pays anything, even attention, to a dusty coffee table. If you're a compulsive housekeeper, then of course you're going to ignore my advice, but if you are feeling guilty because you're not doing what you think someone else thinks you should be doing, then forget it.

I'm not recommending that you turn into a slob. What I am trying to do is absolve you from compulsive housekeeping. I used to be a compulsive housekeeper. I like to call myself a comfortable one now. My aim is to create a comfortable home for my family, not a showcase for other people.

One of the sad, ironic advantages of having no husband is that there is no one you think you are failing when you are less than perfect. You're not disappointing anyone if the place isn't spotless by five P.M. each day. It's unlikely that your children will even notice. I do have one terribly tidy child, grown now, who when she comes home to visit tidies everything in sight until it's out of sight. I can't find anything for days after she's gone. If you have one of these and it's live-in, bear with it and be grateful. Your home will never look like a disaster area.

Guilt, it seems, is an occupational hazard of being a woman. One of the things that is going to happen to you, as you rush about doing what is uppermost and demands to be done, is that you will feel guilty about the less demanding things, including children, that just wait there to be attended to. I'm a prime sufferer myself. I always feel guilty if my kids are working and I'm not, though I find they don't seem to feel at all guilty when I'm up and about and they are stretched out in front of the television set.

If you feel guilty, as I do, about how different, how much more comfortable and secure, their lives might be if you weren't working and neglecting them, stop it. The if-onlies can take you right back to Self-Pity, maudlin variety. Life isn't the same, it never will be, and all the if-onlies in the world won't change it. Be grateful you have your children and think of what character they're building. You're building a little character yourself, and you're going to need it, because women live a long time. Alone.

A little healthy neglect really doesn't hurt a child, not if he learns independence. Bake a pan of brownies once in a while as an unlooked-for bonus. Chocolate addicts like my kids never feel neglected when they're eating brownies.

On the other hand, you mustn't feel like a martyr. It's not only bad for your character; it's also very hard to live with. Give your kids a break as well as yourself. Don't set impossibly high standards that no one can live up to. Break down. Have a little fun once in a while. It'll do you all good.

Your ego is something that you as a widow have to be careful of. It tends to wither, like a flower without sunshine. You have no one to tell you when you're doing a good job or, for that matter, when you're being a darn fool. Lack of feedback can be very damaging to the psyche. You lose your self-image. That's why, whether it's necessary or not, it's actually valuable to a newly single person to go to work. Work guarantees contact with other people. Work can be the biggest morale-lifter you can find. Work provides focus, a chance to get out of the silent house, to become a functioning independent human being in your own right. "Work keeps at bay three great evils," wrote Voltaire, "boredom, vice, and need." A widow would do well to keep all three at bay.

Once in a while, unbidden, a feeling of accomplishment will arise, and this enables you to square your shoulders and keep on keeping on. There's nothing wrong with a little healthy self-congratulation every now and then. It's a whole lot better than guilt. No one ever said you had to be a superlady, but once in a while you feel like it. Go ahead. You're entitled.

❋ 7
Children

> Ring around a rosie,
> A pocket full of posies,
> Husha, husha.
> We all fall down.

NURSERY RHYME

Even in this day and age, protected as we are from death, children know about it, sing about it, play games with it, honor it. This nursery rhyme comes from the time of the Black Death, when sniffing a posy was believed to offer protection against the unseen killer which decimated the population of Europe in the fourteenth century. "We all fall down," of course, means we all die. And we all do, sooner or later.

I believe that adults have no right to hide death from children. It is a terrible thing to lie to them.

I was seven when my grandfather died, and I knew nothing about it. One day I was taken to see grandma's new home, a comfortable apartment, but there was no room for grandpa and no sign of him either.

"What about grandpa?" I remember asking. "Where will he sleep?" And I was told that grandpa had gone away on a long trip and wouldn't be back. What a rotten thing to do, running out on grandma like that! And it was so unlike him. That wasn't fair, not to tell me. I don't remember how old I was before I finally realized grandpa was dead. By the time I knew, he was a fading memory and I was robbed of awe and grief at his death.

Surely with the death of someone as close as a father, there can be no avoidance of the fact. But how well it is handled depends on the age of the child and on the emotional health of the mother. One week after Bill's death, on the Sunday, I drove the children out to the cemetery after church just so we could check in private on what we had left in a crowd at the funeral. The flowers were dead and there was no tombstone.

"Well, there it is," I said. "You see, he's not here. His body is here and we pay it respect."

I do believe that, but I am reminded of a passage in Pearl Buck's book *A Bridge For Passing*, about the death of her husband, in which she recalled her mother's grief at the death of Pearl's brother. A friend said something about the body's being merely the earthly remains, that the child's spirit was safe in heaven. And Pearl's mother replied that the body was all she had left, the body she had borne and nursed and cared for. She has a point. Bill is not in the cemetery; he's closer to me at home, or anywhere I go. But oh, how I miss that body!

Anyway, we didn't have the body to gaze at. We had a muddy pile of earth. Everyone nodded silently at what I had said, and they all looked suitably respectful. We were dry-eyed. Kate broke the silence with a question:

"What's his address?"

We all laughed. Bless her!

"Range 16, lot 43," I said, and we were released.

Laughter can be just as valid a cry of anguish as tears. It's easier (sometimes) to laugh than it is to cry, and it's much more socially acceptable. I know that, but where did my children learn it so young? Laughter is a mask for pain. Sometimes laughter enables you to get closer to the hurtful point than tears ever will. Tears soften and blunt the edges of pain; that's why they are so useful and must be welcomed when they come.

Crying helps. Help your children to cry. Girls and boys. Maybe especially boys, because there still is this stigma attached to masculine tears that they must be helped over. Tears are still the safest release. I'm not saying you have to drown in them, but a few moist eyes early on can brighten the vision later. Help your children to deal with strong feelings. Help them to cry. But laughter makes reality bearable—in short doses—until reality can be faced altogether.

It helps to have a faith at a time like death. Then you can honestly tell your children what you believe, that the soul has left the body and that though we are physically separated from that dear human being, because he is no longer human, we believe and look forward to a time of reunion when we discard our earthly shell. We pray for his spirit and we keep him alive in our memories.

Between the ages of three and five there is an inability to understand death, to conceive of it as a permanent thing. You will be required to give the facts, and to keep on giving them, for as long as the child must hear them. It is a crucial age at which to lose a parent. In a study by psychiatrist Dr. Michael Rutter, reported in Sula Wolff's book *Children Under Stress*, it was found that "the loss of a parent at three or four years is especially damaging because this is the time at which parents are most needed as models for identification."

Somewhere you will have to find a role model for your young sons, perhaps your own brother, if you have one, or brother-in-law, or a cousin, or your father, or a friend of your husband's. At whatever age, sons are terribly vulnerable to their widowed mothers. You must start early to distance yours enough to stand free of you.

Sula Wolff also writes, however, "that the death of a mother generally leads to a greater disruption of the family than the death of a father." If you've been getting the subliminal message from some people that the wrong person died (yes, that too!) tell them that.

Between the ages of five and nine, children develop a gradual acceptance of death as a permanent thing that happens to everyone. They will still want to talk about it a lot. Don't change the subject. Explain the facts. Be open and honest about the cause of death. They will be less frightened than if you shroud it in secrecy.

At this age a child might harbor some feelings of guilt if he or she was ever angry at the deceased. Children have a very direct apprehension of cause and effect and have been known to blame themselves for a death in the family, especially a sudden death, and especially if in the few weeks before the death they happened to have shouted in anger: "I hate you. I wish you were dead." Guilt and fear may get all mixed up in their heads, and you'll have to help them over it. It's important to talk about it.

Then, too, children may feel anger at being left. Why not? Lots of mothers feel angry at being left. It helps to talk about it. He didn't mean to go away and leave you. He couldn't help it. Don't blame him.

And if by chance he did mean it, if he committed suicide, then you still mustn't be angry. Help the children to feel sympathy for the pain and despair and anguish that forced him to such an act. Don't blame him.

But don't blame God either. If you have a faith, find a way to explain death (and life) without implicating God as the villain. If you have honest doubts, express them. Don't be afraid to say, "I don't know." How fortunate you are if you have a strong faith and can communicate your belief to your children!

"God needed him." Have you heard that line? Or—and this is worse—"God punished him." You might not say that one, but pray that your children don't overhear someone else saying it. Death is not a punishment for sin. *Everyone dies.* My husband used to say, "One out of one dies of something," and he was right. Make sure your children understand that.

By the time they're older, children may not turn so freely to their mother to discuss their father's death. It's important that you keep on talking about him—easily and naturally and lovingly. No one else will. People don't seem to want to talk about someone after he dies. It's as if the earth had swallowed him up and he never existed at all. Well, if he didn't exist, where did all these children come from? Stay open. Be accessible. Make sure your children understand that they can talk if they want to talk. Talk a lot. Keep on talking, whatever age they're at. And remember this: Children need large doses of tender loving care.

So do mothers.

Now, having gotten all soft and mushy, let me warn you not to be too soft. Don't cling. Don't smother. Especially your sons. Sula Wolff warns of this: "Clinging mothers, especially to sons, impede the child's growing up process. Some sons can be handicapped by it, too concerned for the widowed mother." Sometimes you have to discourage their concern for you.

One Saturday night that first summer, it happened that both the girls were out, Matt was invited to a friend's for the night, and John was going to a movie. He was the last one out of the house and hesitated as he said good-bye, realizing in the same instant that I would be alone for the evening.

"Would you rather I stayed home?" he asked.

"That's the last thing I want," I said. "Get out of here." You have to do that. In a way, in time, you have to become less of a mother.

It's called being androgynous and it goes hand in hand with becoming the breadwinner, the head of the house, the decision-maker. As you develop your so-called "masculine" qualities of energy, independence, aggressiveness, you will tend to repress the feminine. That's what I mean when I say you become less of a mother. You have to become both mother and father to your children. Again, it isn't easy.

If, however, you have troubles with your children that you feel you cannot handle, there are experts who can help you when the printed word fails and you desperately need to talk to someone. Start with the teacher, if your child is of school age. The teacher knows the kid better than anyone and may be able to help you with your problem. Try your minister, or Sunday school teacher, if you are a regular church attender, or the Scoutmaster or guide leader, if your child attends such a group.

You will discover how very kind other people can be. Different friends have taken my younger son to the Father and Son Banquet at Scouts each year. Both boys' camp directors have been wonderfully kind and helpful. Matt's Big Brother is a joy and a wonder. In fact, the Big Brothers movement is a joy and a wonder, reaching out as it does to help fatherless boys between the ages of six and sixteen. There are times when as a single parent you find it impossible to be in two places at once. That's when friends from many sources step into the breach and help. If never before, you learn to receive gratefully and to say thank you from the bottom of your heart.

If you have a son under sixteen years of age, do try to get a Big Brother for him. The time he gives to your son is valuable to you in more ways than one. When you are responsible for everything your children do, the relief you feel when someone else takes over, if only for a couple of hours, has to be experienced as it cannot be described. The Big Brother may become the role model your child needs and that's really important.

Don't, whatever you do, hold up their missing father as the model your children must live up to. That's blackmail. Don't ever say, "Your father would be disappointed in you." Don't even hint that the child is not living up to his nonexistent father's expectations of him. There is no answer a child can give to that and you have saddled him with guilt and posthumous resentment that he can't get rid of. The only way I conjure up their dead father to my children is in a positive way. I say, "Your father would be proud of you," or, "He'd be happy to see you doing so well."

Tempting as it may be, don't tell your son that he's the man of the house now. Other people will anyway, so you don't have to emphasize it. He'll feel his responsibility keenly as it is; try not to rush him out of childhood any faster than he has already been pushed.

Your children necessarily will assume more responsibility in their lives than they might have. They will be on their own sooner and they will be doing more for themselves—and for you. I can say don't burden your older children with too much responsibility, but it's hard not to. Certainly there is added pressure on them if you have to work to supplement your income. You must rely on your children's cooperation. The danger is that you will lean on them too heavily. Kids are kids and they still have to be respected as such. Sure, they'll pitch in and put dinner in the oven, make a salad, set the table, run errands to the store, clean up after a meal, or help with the cleaning and laundry, and God bless them for it. But don't ask them to make the decisions, plan the menus, or remember what to do without written memory jogs. Or hang up their clothes.

What about money? What provision is there for your dependent children in the event of your death before they are ready to leave the nest? Is your income dependent upon your life or is it in trust or investments that are available to your family as well? Certainly your job income will cease if you should die now, and so would your husband's survivor's pension payable to the widow only. If too many sources were to dry up, then you should consider some insurance to keep your children afloat.

Give a thought to their education, if you can. I gave thought to it, but very little money. In widows' surveys this was the area that altered most dramatically with the death of the father. The fact is that your children will bear more or most, if not all, of the cost of their education themselves. Most states have a system of student loans and grants. Ask at your universities and colleges about the bursaries, loans, grants, scholarships—whatever is available—and ask for application forms. This time, your kids will be doing the asking; it's their future they're asking about. Psychologists have proved that anxiety and tension improve learning ability—another ironic advantage of bereavement.

We have already recognized the fact that bereavement is usually accompanied by a substantial drop in income. This can affect the children in more ways than the obvious one. They are deprived not only of some of the material benefits they had when their father was alive but also of a great deal of their mother's time. Because in her attempts to fill in the money gap she runs out of time for them. There is less money for toys and treats and trips, but there is also less time for inexpensive pleasure outings and for bedtime stories, homework help, and games. In other words, no one is having any fun, least of all you.

That's one of the sadder continuing facts of widowhood. You're not having any fun anymore. The person who made life most interesting for you and with whom you most liked to have fun is gone. No one else is going to go out of his way to see that you have any fun. So you're going to have to manufacture your own.

Your children are going to feel the same way. Not only is half the source of their comfort, well-being, and fun gone, but the one who's left is a lot more sour and serious than they ever remember her being. Small wonder. You were never scared and lonely before. Well, share your loneliness with the kids. Take time to go on a picnic with them or to a movie or to have Chinese food sent in, whatever. Do a jigsaw puzzle, go for a bike ride or cross-country skiing, make popcorn, watch a TV show together, explore a new park. Your solutions need not be expensive. They just have to be done together. You'll find that your children are delightful people to be with, and it's so very comforting to be with people who really love you—very good for the soul and the ego.

Do something else for your children. Have a party. It's good therapy for you and it's good psychology for them. Show them that good times can still happen, even though their father is gone. Have a family sleigh ride, or take a bunch of kids tobogganing or skating and bring them back for hot apple cider and hamburgers or lasagna or something. Or have a backyard barbecue in the summer.

Show your children that you care. Listen to them. Do not judge—"That's a terrible thing to say!" Do not stifle them—"You mustn't think things like that!" Help them to articulate their feelings. Recognize anger if it exists and help them to talk it out. Fear too.

It was several months before Kate and I confessed to each other that every time we burped we waited for eight minutes to see if we would die. Sudden death can leave residual fear like that. Death can happen so easily. You have to learn to trust life again, and help your children to trust, too. Death is not necessarily catching.

Perhaps all of us felt the apprehension that Matthew voiced. He was nervous about leaving me to go back to school the day after the funeral. He was afraid, I guess, that I might drop dead, too, and what was there in his experience to say this might not happen? We all took an extra day off together before we parted to resume our lives again.

Matt is in a Special Education class. I phoned his teacher and warned her of his fear. She discussed his situation with the other children in the class and tried to prepare them for a normal reception of him. It was too much to expect. Not knowing what to say, they said nothing, and avoided him. He came home feeling like a social outcast. Grown-ups also do that, too, say nothing, because they don't know what to say. It's better to speak. Words don't lie as heavy in the air as silence does.

There was only one child who broke the boundaries of fair play with Matt, and I guess he had problems of his own.

81

"Yah, yah," he shouted at Matt one day. "I'm better than you. I have a father and you don't. Yah, yah." That's unanswerable. (But I have the feeling that some women think that about me and my lack of a husband.)

Children, in short, will go through the same stages of shock, rage, fear, and withdrawal that their bereaved mother does. If you can help them through it, you will perhaps not only shorten their mourning period; you may also help yourself. As a widow, of course, you are harder hit than your children. You have lost the companion of your life, your mate, your lover, your best friend (haven't you?). Your grief will affect the whole household, and will continue to do so when you have attacks of it.

Oddly enough, however, or perhaps not oddly at all, just as a widow who has survived an unhappy marriage will be more badly affected by the death of her husband, so will her children be less able to handle the bereavement. Again, it is the grief and guilt of the mother that affect the children. If you have such a problem you'll have to work out your hostility for the sake of your own mental health, but I pray that you do not turn your hostility on the children. They need you, as whole and loving as you can be.

You must learn to share with your children—your sorrow, satisfactions, some of your worries, your self—without leaning on them too heavily. Their lives have changed, too; you can't protect them from the world anymore. The world has already happened to them. Go ahead and communicate with them, and expect a lot. They can deliver more help, common sense, and practical solutions than you could have imagined. Just don't frighten them. You're the adult; keep it that way. You make the decisions. Inform them of your plans, but don't expect them to plan for you. You can't opt out that easily. You're the head of the household now. Act like it.

Now if I sound awesomely tough and mature, let me quickly confess that there have been many times when I have broken down and been the recipient of comfort from my children. My youngest leaves his place at the table and comes and pats my arm if he sees weather warnings in me. In the first weeks and months when I continued to try to take the walks Bill and I were accustomed to taking on Sunday afternoons, Matt would leave his friends and run after me to tag along. And the older children would spot my lonely times and one or the other of them would wander into the living room and offer to talk. I have learned more about electronics and stereo equipment and physics from John than I care to know. But they also help more with chores than they ever did and provide companionship as well as assistance. There is a kind of bittersweet compensation in this. They don't have to share me with my husband anymore. Perhaps that is a saving grace, that although they no longer have two parents, they now have access to the undivided attention of one—when they can catch me.

One other thing I have to bring up: dating. That is an old-fashioned word, and there is much more said about it in another chapter, but you should give a thought to how it affects the children, because it will in turn affect you. Little children often feel threatened by their mother's dating. They are afraid she will be taken away from them, or else they resent a father figure, if the man in question attempts to come on too strong as an authority. Teenaged children feel threatened too, particularly a boy who regards himself in some way as the man of the house.

As for Mother, she feels like an overgrown teenager herself. Very odd. I mean, theoretically, you can stay out as late as you want, because you're grown-up and you don't have a curfew, but can you really face your kids if you stay out till four in the morning? I can't. I'm still the mother.

Children older than mine feel somewhat proprietary about their widowed mothers. A few I have spoken to are genuinely happy for their parent when she finds another interest, whether it's a round-the-world cruise, a good job, or a new husband. But many adult children are fearful that a new man in their mother's life is merely after her money—I mean, he couldn't possibly be interested in her in a man-woman relationship, could he? (He could.) The commonest reaction to a new man is a well-hidden, latent jealousy. An older widow's decision to remarry can bring back painful memories of the bereavement that left her thus available. As long as she was faithful to her husband's memory, father was still around, in a way. Even at this late stage in life, a son or daughter may feel rejected by the mother's insistence on having a life of her own. If any of these reactions occur in your life, you will find they're harder to deal with than with the bewildered grief of a five-year-old. But you will have to deal with the problem. All I can say is, keep the lines of communication open.

Your relationship with your grown children is at once a personal and a contemporary problem. The extended family of past generations is no longer popular. Widowed grandmothers and maiden aunts and dotty uncles and spinster sisters used to live together and share the child care chores with the mother and father in houses big enough to accommodate all of them. Daughters and sons today are not too eager to have a widowed mother live with them in smaller quarters, and she is often fiercely independent and wants to do for herself in her own place as long as she can. It's not an easy problem to solve. Each situation is individual. Your arrangements will depend on your financial situation, your health, and your relationship with your children.

"It's harder for older widows," an older widowed aunt wrote to me, "than for young ones, for you are still needed. That is the most difficult adjustment to make—to have no one to whom you are absolutely essential." She is right. I am lucky that I have not yet been left alone, but I know the time is coming. There have been many times already when I have been aware that I need my children more than they need me, and I know I must not let that need overwhelm them. If I seem at this point to be suggesting more problems than I can solve, the fault is not in me but in the situation we find ourselves in. It's a bind.

One by one my children left home, though they come back regularly for food and comfort. I'm beginning to feel like the last of the Ten Little Indians. But I have not been as disturbed by the departure of the fledglings from the nest as other women I know. One mother said to me when our first daughters went off to college: "Isn't it terrible, that empty place at the dinner table?" I didn't remind her I already had an empty place.

I have not been as disturbed because I have this larger departure I am still coping with. At least my children are still on this earth. I can phone them and they can visit and I can talk to them. And hug them. That helps.

What you do for your children is what you must do for yourself. Face the facts. Reality hurts, but hiding from it is going to hurt more in the long run. Share your sorrow. Support each other in your grief. Your children, no matter what their ages, are the only people in the world who come close to knowing how bad it is, who have a loss almost as deep as yours. Care for them and share yourself. If you can, share faith and hope as well. Assert your faith by making an effort. Try to make things *better* for your children because of the insight you've gained. Love them and thereby honor the person whose loss you share.

❀ 8
Sex and the single widow

So far as is known, no widow ever eloped.

E. W. HOWE

Walk through any cemetery with tombstones in it dating from before the turn of the century and you will see the social change that has led to the situation of widows in North America today. In the dim dark days before antisepsis, women often died in childbirth, so it was not uncommon for a man to outlive two or three wives. A man can still have two or three wives, but it's called divorce and it's much more messy and expensive. Now women are outliving men because someone thought of washing his hands before delivering a baby.

And then there's the death wish of the North American male, expressed in expense accounts, high living, not enough exercise, too many business pressures. If the feminist movement manages to relieve men of some of the pressures and responsibilities of making it in the world today and thereby enables them to live a little longer and keep women company a little longer, that would be a great achievement.

Because women today face, increasingly, a great portion of their lives without men.

One in six women over the age of eighteen is a widow; that means ten million women. The average age at which a woman is widowed is fifty-six; the average life expectancy of a woman born today is 77.5 years. But if a woman is sixty-five today, she has a life expectancy of another 18.4 years. Among widows in their twenties who have two children, 76.6 percent remarry, while only 44.8 percent of those in their thirties also with two children remarry. According to the social scientists I have talked to, fewer than one in ten widows ever remarry. Any way you look at it, they have a long time to go on alone. Well-meaning friends have told you (haven't they?) that you will get married again in a few years, as if that were the solution to all your problems. You know it isn't. Married people have problems, too. But you have to realize that widows are a glut on the market. Everyone may assume that you'll get married again, but you mustn't assume that. As with your insurance policies, you must consider your options. Marriage is merely one of them, perhaps the least likely.

But you should think about it. Work your way through it and come to a decision so that you are whole and secure within yourself. Think about whether you want to risk your emotions and your life on another marital venture. One widow wrote me: "I have not yet met a man with whom I want to spend more than three or four hours—the length of time it takes to eat a good dinner."

There are several stereotypes about widows: there is the Biblical widow, poor and sorrowing, with her widow's mite and her struggle to survive. There is the sex-mad, wealthy widow of a simpler society (Shakespeare's plays are full of eager widows), when widows were not such a bad catch. If a widow had children, she had proved her fertility and ability to survive childbirth when it was still economically advantageous to have children. She usually had some property or money, never a bad thing, and her sexual expertise had to be assumed. Today sexual expertise is rampant, widows are a glut on the market, and wealthy ones are rare.

By Victorian times, following the lead of the widowed queen who went into a state of paralysis after Albert died, widows were swathed in black and left high, dry, respectable, and neglected in cold parlors with other widows (they have so much in common!), their sewing and their grandchildren to occupy them. They were supposed to live on their memories and be grateful.

A combination of these attitudes still exists about widows. Widows are supposed to be retroactive vestal virgins, keeping alight the memorial candle and protecting the flame of fidelity even after death has parted the twain. It's not fair, of course.

I speak to a lot of widows in the course of my work and I seem to hear more every year to reinforce my conviction that it's unfair, that the ghetto we've been thrust into is stifling, that the expectation that we will live out the remainder of our lives in uncomplaining celibacy is harsh and unfeeling. No one puts black wreaths on the door anymore; why should we have black veils swathed around our sexuality? We do it to ourselves, too.

It may be an insoluble problem, however. At least recognize that it *is* a problem. Don't comfort yourself that only 32 percent of widows are under the age of sixty-five and that the other 68 percent don't have a problem. That's another stereotype: the blue-haired sixty-five-year-old widow with her rings and her poodle, content to eat and gossip and live out her life on the vicarious kicks and lollipop thrills of Harlequin romances. Hah.

The double standard of aging is very hard on widows. Shere Hite, in her best-selling study of women's sexuality *The Hite Report*, says: "For centuries it has been a hideous cliché in our culture that older women are not sexual women." Society would prefer to believe that older women are asexual. Women know better. Even when they are well past the menopause, women still see themselves as sensual, sexual human beings. According to the women surveyed in *The Hite Report,* the enjoyment of sex heightens and the capacity for it increases with age. Women in their late sixties and early seventies reported both interest and aptitude. As the greeting card puts it more truly than Hallmark realizes: "You're not getting old, dearie, you're getting better!" But what good does it do you if you're alone?

While mature men are not blamed for taking young wives, an older woman—that is, any woman over forty—is supposed to be grateful if a spry seventy-year-old gives her the nod. I actually had one call a radio station where I was doing an open line show to propose marriage because he needed someone to cook and clean for him. "What are you offering in return?" I asked. As Susan Sontag put it in her devastating essay *The Double Standard of Aging,* "a woman knows that should she re-enter the sexual market at a later date—because of divorce, or the death of her husband or the need for erotic adventure—she must do so under a handicap far greater than any man of her age (*whatever* her age may be) and regardless of how good-looking she is."

Not that widows don't get sexual offers. They do, but they're generally from married men. A whole survey could be devoted to the lines men use with widows. It's a different approach. The general theme is selflessness. Any widow will tell you (they've told *me*) that the male attitude toward a widow is purely altruistic, although men do tend to expect more than their due of gratitude for whatever services they offer. Most men, in fact, are surprised when most widows say no. *No thank you.* They like to think of themselves as social workers performing a needed service. Sexual social workers.

One gets offers from the most bizarre sources, leading one to suspect that the motivation is not really pity but the prospect of a new kick. Not that it's easy to storm the bastions. Widows are highly vulnerable and they can sometimes be taken once or twice because of that vulnerability, but they get gun-shy pretty fast.

The first time I had hands laid on me in lust and not in love, I cried a lot. Forgotten tremors can trigger responses that are difficult to control. They have, however, a therapeutic effect. They complete the sexual mourning process.

"There is no sanctuary," wrote Cyril Connolly, "in one bed from the memory of another." One widow reported to me that she couldn't reach a climax with her first post-husband lover. She loved the loving and the cuddling, but she just couldn't let go. Remember the film *A Man and a Woman?* A divorced man and a widow who think they have fallen in love try to go to bed, but she finds she can't make it. The memory of her husband—more than memory—his imprint is all over her body. She cries, and he withdraws, helpless and defeated by a ghost. When one has been married for a long time, one retains a married psyche. It takes a while to become a single woman again, no longer a wife. Perhaps that is one reason why widows, even though they are lonely, hold out. Sociologist Paul Bohannan estimates that one-fifth of widows and one-tenth of divorcees experience more than three years' abstinence before resuming sexual relationships. Widows, particularly, feel they are being faithful to a memory and find it difficult to take that first giant step into an alien bed.

I know it's fear. My own wound is still so raw I am terrified of what another loss could do to me. I think I can stand anything, and I can, but why put myself out for such pain? I found that my feeling has been duly recognized by psychiatrists. It is called a "phobic response to marriage" and is experienced by women who lost their mates without warning. It affects the nature of eventual recovery. Yes.

But you still need companionship. Fortunate are you if you can find someone who will be satisfied with the lemonade kisses and milk-and-water hugs of your youth, that is, a platonic companion. And fortunate, too, if that's all *you* want. Try as one will to live a spiritual life, one still has a physical body that is comforted by human contact. It's another of the inexorable problems of widowhood that must be dealt with. Obviously, you're not going to be able to live with yourself in a state of promiscuity (are you?) but you have this devastating hunger. . . .

If and when a widow starts seeing other men, she must overcome a feeling of disloyalty. She has no one left to be faithful to, and that is a disconcerting realization. It's as if she has lost her anchor, her touchstone, her safety zone—all of that. "I want someone to hold me," one young widow wrote to me, and her feeling is shared by most widows. It isn't always a sexual feeling. It's the need to be cradled and comforted, to be hugged. I'm not the only one who goes around saying how necessary hugs are for human beings. But sex is important, too.

"Widows are so gullible," an older widow wrote, "that anything in pants looks good after a while!"

One's needs, after all, must be reconciled with one's morality. It depends on one's personal attitudes (and religion) as to which is easier to bear—guilt or frustration. Often religion serves only to complicate matters, not to resolve them. One widow came up to me after a seminar I was conducting on companionship and second marriages.

"My doctor says I should have an affair," she said, "that it would do me a world of good. I told my minister that and he said, 'you know what our religion thinks of that.' What should I do?" She was asking me a direct question I hadn't yet learned how to handle for myself. I told her what the semanticist Korzybski said: "God may forgive you, but your nervous system won't." That didn't help much, I guess, but it's true. In the end, you have to do what you are comfortable with. You have to give yourself permission to behave according to what makes you most comfortable, whether it's celibacy or not. You're the one you have to live with.

Some widows, of course, hope to remarry. I used to think I would. I was good at marriage, I thought, having had a successful one. But many of the men I met weren't good at it, being battle-scarred and scared survivors of messy divorces. Trust doesn't come so easily in that case, and pain does. The few widowers I met were victims of great expectations or of bad timing.

Timing truly is everything, for all concerned. It is quite true that most widows get more offers (but not of marriage) than they ever accept. That's almost another cliché. But the offers they accept get little acknowledgment. Most of them are horror stories.

The horror lies in the fact that the two principals want different things. The widow, like all women, wants tender loving care, some undivided attention, concern and affection, not necessarily marriage. The man wants something else. He claims to be helping her, but it is really himself he is servicing.

The one fact that emerges again and again, from all the stories I hear, is that a widow can't be too careful. It wouldn't be a bad idea for a widow to get a credit rating on every man she goes out with, and I'm talking about character, not money—though it wouldn't be so dumb to check out his finances, too.

I have learned of widows who signed over their businesses, their houses, their housekeeping services, and their bodies to fast, sweet-talking men who were going to look after them. I know one widow, a younger woman, who had actually moved in with a man and his three children. He was in the process of getting a divorce, he said, so he could marry her. She was housekeeper and babysitter and mistress. He then asked her to move out but come in by the day for the child-care, so he could list her as a housekeeper and not jeopardize the divorce proceedings. Well, he got his divorce and promptly got married—to someone else.

Another widow wrote me that she had had four affairs since her husband's death three years earlier, including a fairly lengthy one with a divorced man who moved into her house with his children. Hers and his fought.

There's another consideration. Even if a widow is prepared to take a chance herself, she must think about her children, especially if they are still at home. Personally, I don't like the thought of waking up in the morning and introducing the children to the man in bed beside me, nor would I be any happier to be the strange lady in some daddy's bed, ready for a spurious togetherness at a family breakfast. I don't have that much poise.

Another widow I know met a charming divorced man (there may be a shortage of widowers, but there's no shortage of divorced men these days). She noticed that when he played with his children, invariably one or the other of them got hurt, painfully, to the point of tears. It was always accidental but it happened with surprising frequency. He didn't seem to know his own strength or how to curtail it in horseplay with his little ones. Then, by chance, my acquaintance met a woman who was a friend of the man's ex-wife, so close a friend, in fact, as to have been the one who took her in when her husband beat her up. A widow—or any woman, for that matter—has the right to expect that a man she goes out with hasn't hit a woman since he was in sixth grade.

I know widows who have met men at singles' bars and I know a couple who have advertised in the personal column for a companion. There is one little catch to men you meet without any background information from friends or business associates: they're often married. Not unhappily married, either. Happily married and happily looking around.

The moral to all my stories is that it pays to ask questions. Find out. Do a little sleuthing. Make sure you know something about the man before you get hurt or taken or both. Don't go out with a perfect stranger. Remember, no one is perfect. These truths may seem self-evident, but not to a woman long sheltered and newly thrust into a world of singles.

I have never tried a singles' bar myself, or the personal column, but I have met a number of men at friends' houses. Even with a proper introduction in a safe and respectable setting, you still have to be careful. Your friends don't have to be as discriminating as you are. "Dining," as Edna Ferber once observed, "is not mating."

Not that a widow is mating. Far from it. Most of the time she's scared, tired, and reticent. She is not all that eager to raise someone else's children or, if she has come through a terminal illness with her spouse, to nurse another man to his grave. All thoughts of marriage aside, even conversation is difficult. Ten, fifteen, twenty years of marriage spoil one for casual conversations. With a new man there are no comfortable assumptions, no backlog of shared experiences, no tolerance for each other's foibles. "It's easy to make new friends," a friend once said to me, "but hard to make old ones." It's even harder to make old husbands; you had to start several years ago. You did, in fact.

Conversation. Pillow talk. It isn't merely sex that is missing from the lives of women alone. It's friendship, affection, spiritual intimacy—all much more difficult to replace than mere physical contact. Widows who have nursed their husbands through a long illness and who were denied any physical release because of the illness—anywhere from three months to six years—tell me they didn't feel the sexual hunger during that period that they do now that their husbands are gone. They still had a companion and some physical contact, the comfort of a kiss, a hug, or a pat, or a hand held in silent understanding.

Many of the women quoted in *The Hite Report* corroborate this need for touching, for friendly physical contact, for a little loving, a little warmth to make one feel less alone. We're all alone, of course, but widows are more alone, or feel more alone.

But there's a reticence about physical contact in our society. Says Shere Hite, "Aside from touching one's partner during sex, it only seems possible to touch children and animals." So we're back to the stereotype of the blue-rinse widow lavishing her affection on her poodle or her cats, and the loving grandmother eagerly babysitting all her grandchildren in return for hugs and kisses. It's an acceptable way of expressing a need and at least partially fulfilling it.

So for the widow, even touching is out in an age when sex is in. Since our society today is so very sex-oriented, celibacy seems to be the drastic and difficult alternative for widows. Women in *The Hite Report* varied in their response to celibacy from a sense of strength and independence to feelings of frustration, rejection, and depression.

I know celibacy never hurt anyone, although the French writer Remy de Gourmont once called it "the last perversion." Nevertheless, I do not accept my imposed celibacy easily, nor does any widow I know but one. This one told me she had absolutely no sense of loss as far as sex was concerned. She had never enjoyed it much and thought her husband felt the same way, for they were happily married for twenty-seven years. After his death, when she prepared to move, she came across a trunk in the basement and found inside it a collection of pornography and an account of her husband's affairs that took her breath and faith away for a time. However, she accepted her own responsibility for this secret life of her husband's and came to terms with it. For the present without him, although she missed his companionship, she didn't miss sex at all. I told her I envied her that peace.

I have a great sex drive and it drives me up the wall. I think sex is one of the nicest adult games there is, between very close, loving friends, preferably husband and wife, though I have come so far in my thinking as to recognize other relationships. The pleasure of another's mouth and hands and arms is addictive.

I always believed in a) chastity and b) fidelity. I married young and fidelity was easy. Chastity is not. But I am of a generation of women who were taught, and most of whom still believe, that the sex act without love is worse than nothing. The physical movements are the external gestures of an emotional and spiritual state called love. With love the gestures are meaningful; without love they are degrading.

"I went away for a weekend with a man," one not-so-merry widow told me, "thinking I was very free and grown-up. But Monday morning was worse than ever and I hated myself as well."

Another told me she had tried sex-as-release twice and found it hopelessly dissatisfying. "When it's over you miss love," she said.

So I maintain as I did in the dear sheltered days of my one-man marriage that sex without commitment is futile. Harder for me to say now, with my nose pressed against the glass of the candy store, wanting what I haven't got.

There's lots of understanding counsel at your nearest library these days. For instance, Dr. Frieda Porat, a marriage and family counselor at the Center of Creativity and Growth in Palo Alto, California, has written a book called *Changing Your Lifestyle*. She comments on the pressures implicit in meeting new people: "It is not always fun to meet new people, to charm a new acquaintance, to communicate your availability, to experience rejections, or to compete for friendship, attention and love. A person has to have not only great reserves of energy but also great self-confidence to sustain a continuous search for new relationships."

And widows are not certain of the kind of relationship they want. It's still easiest, perhaps, to say they miss sex and to search for that, and a lot of widows do. Sex is the name of the game these days, the game you have to play to get the other things a widow wants more: comfort, companionship, cuddling—in short, love. Love is much harder to find than sex.

Ingrid Bengis, author of *Combat in the Erogenous Zone,* said, "When I love no one it is the absence of love that is more painful than the absence of sex."

I suppose it depends on who you are and where you've been, and maybe how old you are. Widows who have had a good marriage know how important love is, but widows who have had a good marriage also know how important sex is.

And we haven't mentioned sin, have we? Sin is an old-fashioned word these days, to anyone but religious nuts, people think. It happens that I am a Christian, a practicing one. I'm not very good at it, but I keep practicing. So I believe in sin, and I'd like to avoid it if I can, but it's not easy. I am comforted by what St. Augustine said so long ago: "Lord, grant me chastity and continence, but do not grant them yet."

On the other hand, he also said, "Second marriages are lawful, but holy widowhood is better." Catch 22.

And what about this terrible, relentless hunger that will not go away? I have talked to women in their seventies who still feel it. There seems to be no easy solution, not for the millions of women already widowed.

You're going to be all right. Bertrand Russell suggests that women will atrophy and become brittle if they give up sex after having had it for years. David Reuben (of *Everything You Always Wanted to Know about Sex* fame) says much the same thing. They're both talking nonsense. There is nothing to get brittle, or rusty, for that matter. If your general health is good, so are your moving parts. You'll be able to deliver if and when you want to. But your own needs must be recognized. Why do you think older widows lavish so much love and affection on their dogs or cats? And babysit and teach Sunday school and go to church? All these are acceptable ways of letting off—and receiving—love.

Hugs and kisses are available closer to home when you still have children there. I asked for it, for loving. My older son, at fourteen, was embarrassed the first time I asked him to give me a hug. Matthew, my younger son, never had any problem, because he had never stopped. And my daughters' shoulders seemed at times too young for the burden of grief I was laying on them. But my need for physical reassurance was strong and I got my hugs.

I think it's good for the children. Two of mine are not demonstrative by nature, but they can handle a swift hug with a great deal more aplomb now. It has proved to be a helpful expertise for them to have. And it helped me to sublimate a need.

Sublimate, according to the dictionary, means "to convert the energy of primitive impulses into acceptable social and cultural manifestations." Fortunately these days a lot more manifestations are acceptable than ever used to be! It's more likely that the limits of your behavior lie within you and not in the acceptance of society around you.

You still have to convert that energy and find an outlet for those impulses. Exercise helps, in more ways than one. Regular exercise is going to keep you fit and healthy into your old age, and you need every resource you can lay your hands on. Join a club or a Y, take yoga classes, pursue a sport on your own. Just make sure that you get enough good, hard, regular exercise to convert that energy. If you ever do decide that sublimation is for the birds, you'll find you have stamina for other things also.

Cherish your friends. I am a closer, better friend to a lot of people than I ever was in my married life. I need them, and they have made room for me in their lives. But I try to give in return. Marriage, you see, isn't the only close relationship you can have.

Widowhood, it seems, is becoming a complete personality course. A finishing school? As you gather all your resources you become a more complete, self-fulfilling person, never a bad thing. One widow actually said to me, "Isn't it ironic that I had to lose my husband to find myself?" Life is full of such irony.

So you gain strength as you go along, and perspective and new, wider, extended friendships. And the best new friend you have is yourself.

9
Loneliness

> *There are days when solitude for someone my age
> is a heady wine that intoxicates you with freedom,
> others when it is a bitter tonic, and still others
> when it is a poison that makes you beat your
> head against the wall. . . . This evening I would
> much prefer not to say which it is; all I want is
> to remain undecided, and not to be able to say
> whether the shiver that will seize me when I
> slip between the cold sheets comes from fear or
> contentment.*
>
> COLETTE

Loneliness is an increasing problem today and is not con-
fined to widows. The high mobility of our society has made
deep and lasting friendships difficult to make and maintain.
If a couple doesn't have each other, they're in trouble, and
frequently they are, as the increasing fragmentation of the
family makes clear. There is no doubt, however, that inti-
mate relationships alleviate loneliness. We all know that.
We also know that the relationships have to be creative and
supportive and based on genuine affection, or they will be
damaging. Still, drowning people clutch at straws. It is loneliness that causes a lot of so-called promiscuity among
single people (and not only singles!). Sex can provide a
short-term spurious intimacy that begins by comforting and
ends by alienating people even more. The moral is that we
all need love.

This book is really about love. Death wouldn't mean anything if you hadn't loved the one who died. And you are not
going to survive now if you do not withdraw that love and

aim it elsewhere. Your first target is yourself. If you don't love and accept yourself, you're not going to be able to love others, and you're going to go on being lonely.

First you have to find out who you are. You've been someone else all your life. You were your parents' daughter, your husband's wife, your children's mother. Now you are your own keeper, and a survivor. In spite of all the kindnesses of well-meaning friends and relatives, the one thing they can't do for you is make you grow. In fact, they have a tendency to make you become less than you could be, precisely because they are so kind and well-meaning.

When you lose your husband, you lose your best friend and your sternest critic as well. Lots of people tell you when you look nice, when you've done a good job, when your dessert is delicious, or what a good speech you made. But few people care enough to tell you when you've been a horse's ass. They just let you go on making a fool of yourself. Surely you did that for each other, rode herd, provided a system of checks and balances, offered constructive criticism, blew the whistle when it was time? I hope you did. And that's what you miss when you don't have it anymore—feedback. You have to learn to look at yourself.

Know yourself. It's an ancient Greek saw, and it still has a few teeth. Take a good long look at yourself. Pain will have removed a few scales from your eyes, and you should be able to see more clearly. Ask yourself a few questions.

Are you drinking too much? Sorry, but this is a trap a lot of widows fall into: I know several, especially ones who have been well provided for financially. With no pressures driving them out to work, forcing them to focus on something other than themselves, and with no one suffering economically if they spend too much money on booze, they wallow in self-pity and whiskey. And most of their friends are too soft-hearted to tell them to snap out of it. Indulgence is not always kind; self-indulgence is downright destructive. Drinking alone and too much is an unproductive activity.

You're being a damn fool if that's what you're doing. Stop it.

Quit drinking. Get a job. Go read to a shut-in. Take a trip. Clean your own house. Have a grandchild. Take a Great Books Course. Have an affair!

Which brings us to the next hard question. Are you screwing around? Are you getting known as an easy lay? Are you being, in other words, promiscuous? In Bermuda, there is an expression for this kind of behavior, which is often characteristic of frantic, frightened widows. It's called "going foolish." Everyone knows you're not in your right mind, but at least try to hang on to your body. Don't go foolish.

Widows are highly vulnerable. I'll be the first to admit that. It's all too easy to drift in and out of one affair after the other, searching for love and picking up a little easy loving. There are a lot of lonely people out there, willing to be partners. And your friends, if they realize what you're doing, will continue to be kind. They'll forgive you, or refuse to judge you in the first place, and point instead to what you've been through, poor dear. You're going to have to be your own judge.

You think you have nothing left to lose, but you have. It's called self-respect. Decide what you want most, then figure out what to do about it.

There are four kinds of relationships, according to psychologists, that mitigate against loneliness. The first is the romantic sexual relationship. If you can rule that one out, at least for the time being, there are still three others that you can work on. These are friendships, family relationships, and personal commitment to a cause, a course of action, a community, a productive type of work, or a social network of some kind. All these are other-directed. Once you have truly learned to love yourself you can turn your capacity for love, tenderness, care, and concern toward others. And you'll make more friends, almost more than you'll have time for; I guarantee it!

There is a difference between loneliness and being alone. Being alone can get to be a habit, a delightful one. Being alone can give you freedom to do what you want; call it self-indulgence if you will. Being alone can encourage self-development and self-reliance as well, both valuable attributes to have. But an attack of loneliness is an assault on your whole system and on the whole careful structure of self-protectiveness you have set up. Though it may occur less and less frequently as time passes, when an attack does come on, like a tidal wave, the shock can carry you gasping and breathless and sobbing right back to the beach where you were first stranded.

First of all, be comforted; it happens to every widow. Next, what are you going to do about it? All your hard-won strength has got to be of some use to you now when you need it. In this list-happy, pragmatic world we live in, there are lots of things you can do about it. Consider:

1. Make a list. Write down the times when your loneliness strikes and take measures to prevent the next attack. Frequently it's seasonal and you can't do much about it. Anniversaries, birthdays, Christmas, Thanksgiving, private milestones in your life together—these can trigger attacks year after year. Widows who become grandmothers long after their husband's death tell me that the birth may cause retroactive pain. I find weddings very painful. As I say, there's not much you can do about something as inexorable as the calendar, except maybe brace yourself, and know that this, too, will pass.

But there are other lists you can make, happier ones. Make a list of dinner parties you'd like to have and list the people you'd invite and plan the menus. You may get around to one or none of them, but you've had the time-consuming pleasure of planning them. Make a list of all your clothes, from memory, and then make a list of ones you should get rid of and ones you can add something to so that they'll last another season. Make a list of new clothes you'd like to buy. Now make a list of clothes you can afford to buy! You can make Christmas shopping lists in July if you really get going. Once you get the hang of it, you don't need me to help you.

2. Paint a room, or a piece of furniture, or a picture.

3. Clean your oven.

4. Polish the silver.

5. With everything so clean, have a party!

6. Cook up a storm—for your party.

7. But if you can't afford to have a party, try cooking something you've never cooked before, something really complicated and creative. Even if you don't feel like eating it when you've done, you had the fun and concentration of doing it.

8. Sew something spectacular. For me it's spectacular if I sew on a button, but I know women who enjoy the challenge of a French couturier design pattern.

9. Do something you've never done before. Make it something you've always had a secret desire to do. Obviously there are financial limitations to this. It isn't likely you can take off on a trip around the world. But maybe you've always been meaning to explore an art gallery and never got around to it. Or take in a local ferry boat ride, or train ride, or some equally obvious local tourist attraction that natives never get around to doing. Do it.

10. Take a trip. Invite yourself somewhere. You must have had friends invite you to come and visit. Take them up on it. You needn't stay long. But a visit with friends will give you a real lift and is guaranteed to dispel loneliness.

11. Write something: a poem? a letter? a diary? That's best of all. As a writer I am addicted to paper, but anyone with a fresh pad of paper and a ball-point pen can write down what she feels and get it out where she can look at it. That's how Lynn Caine, author of the bestseller *Widow*, which you should read, began to write her book. I find a diary is cheaper than a shrink and it helps to distance the pain a little.

12. Cut your hair, or color it, or both. Remember that

line from Wilde's *The Importance of Being Ernest?* "I hear her hair has turned quite gold from grief." I'm not being as facetious as I sound. Have a facial, a pedicure, a massage. Pamper yourself, in other words. Do something to make yourself feel good, and to feel good about yourself.

13. Turn your electric blanket on high and go back to bed. Scunge. One widow wrote me that she used to watch the *TV Guide* and when there was a movie she really wanted to see on the Morning Movie, she would take a breakfast tray back to bed with her and watch it. Why not?

14. Take a course. Join a political party and work for it actively. Read a book. You may pamper your body, but you should give your mind a good workout. Take your mind off your troubles and set it other problems.

15. But give your body a workout, too. Take up a new sport, or go back to an old one. Take tennis lessons. Start jogging. Swim a mile.

16. Make love. This has its complications and draw-backs, which we have already discussed.

17. Get out of the house. Go to a movie or a singles bar (drink pop if you're nervous). Go on a picnic. Take an historic walk. Go to a concert. Explore something.

18. Crawl into a hole and pull the hole in after you. Sometimes it's so bad that's all you can do. Well, go ahead and brood. Wallow in it. Cry. Feel sorry for yourself. But don't try to share this with anyone. When you're fit for human companionship again, emerge, like a butterfly from a grubby cocoon. Have a hot bath—with bubbles—and you're bound to feel better in half an hour.

19. Scream.

20. Pray.

21. Forgive someone. There's a lot of residual anger flying around in you. When you're in one of these moods pick out someone you really feel resentful of and forgive him or her. Do something for her: bake her a loaf of bread or invite her for lunch or write her a note. Freed of even a fraction of your burden of anger, you will feel much much better.

22. Make fudge with a child. If you don't have one the right age, borrow one.

23. Get organized. Getting organized takes a lot of time and can usually get you involved enough to tide you over an attack. You can organize your files—you must have files of something you want organized! Sort out your recipes. Save things. Throw things out. Go through all your magazines. Clip things. Write things down. Oh, this will make you feel better!

24. Start a clippings collection: happy or comforting or challenging, poems, quotations, thoughtful letters from people, news items, encouraging words, cartoons, whatever. Paste them in a scrapbook. Then when you're down you can reread them. That's why people hang posters like one I found which reads:

> I believe in the sun
> Even when it is not shining
> I believe in love
> Even when I am alone
> I believe in God
> Even when He is silent.

25. Go through it. You have to, you know. There's no turning back.

You will have realized, going through this list, that most of the solutions assume a certain amount of energy on your part. What happens if the spirit is young but the flesh is aging and weak? Loneliness is a problem compounded by age. It takes get-up-and-go to make loneliness get up and go. And sometimes it takes money too, more money than you have. There must be ways that an older person can find to ease the bad days without it costing an arm and a leg, or using tired ones. What can you do?

If society tends to ignore widows generally, it especially neglects older ones, trapped by frailty in a lonely room. Unoccupied time hangs heavy, and you are the one who must fill it, moment by moment, day by day.

I knew a woman, a widow, who was trapped by arthritis in a room where she was brought three not-always-inspired meals a day. People who visited her came away with a lift, and so they went back again. She listened to them; she didn't complain about her own aches and pains, which were myriad and severe. She remembered their children's names, and their husbands', and asked after them. She was glad to see them when they came and never referred to how long it had been since she saw them last, if indeed it was a long time. She appreciated whatever was done for her and made her visitor and benefactor feel like a queen for being so gracious and kind and generous. She made it very easy for people to love her. They wanted to see her again, so they did.

That woman was my mother.

I am not a TV addict myself—in fact, I rarely watch television—but I bless it daily for the pleasure it brought my mother and all shut-ins. I don't know what Mother would have done without her TV families, all the people in the soaps in whose lives she got involved, to say nothing of the hockey and football games she got so excited about.

And she did crossword puzzles and double acrostics until they came out of her ears. Some women knit; my mother puzzled. She had a mind like a steel trap. I guess I can face pain and aging, failing health and weakening flesh. ("Old age," wrote an aunt of mine, "is not for sissies.") But God grant me my wits. And you yours.

You haven't lived all this time for nothing. You have a few foxy things you can still do. If you can't get out and see the world, then you can get the world to come and see you.

Most centers have mobile library services, which include taking books to shut-ins, but it depends on the library funding in your area. You'll have to check it out, and you might be the one to agitate for such a service, if it doesn't exist. The idea is that if you can't get to the library for your books, you get the library to come to you. If you still enjoy reading, you get a bonus, but even if you don't, or just want to look at the pictures, at least you have a human being coming to you—bearing books. If you're blind, the library may bring you tapes of books to listen to. This service may also be available through the National Federation of the Blind, with its fifty thousand members and fifty state and four hundred local organizations.

If you have a faith, and most people do, whether or not it bears the title of a religion, you can pray a lot. But if you believe in organized religion as well, you're ahead of the game. Make sure your name is still on the lists of whatever church or temple you belonged to, keep up your dues (offering), and you'll be on the visiting list. That means that once or twice or several times a year some of the more active women of the church will bring you flowers left over from a special service or tea, and the minister might even drop in to check on your spiritual progress—and that all makes for more visitors to darken your doorstep and lighten your life.

Inquire about physiotherapy treatments. You probably need them, anyway. Ask your doctor if he would recommend them. A young physiotherapist coming in once or twice a month can do wonders for your morale as well as for your muscles and you may be able to get the service on your Medicare, if you are an older citizen, or Medicaid, if yours is a low-income household.

Similarly, if you're too weak to wash your own hair now, or need some other specific personal help (it's hard to reach over to cut your toenails, too), check out home care. There is a National Association for Home Care, but you will have to find out the rules in your own state regarding home care and supplemental nursing services. Enlightened governments are beginning to realize that it is cheaper to support such supplemental services and enable older people to remain in their homes as long as they can than to ship them off to expensive (and impersonal) nursing and senior citizen homes.

There are also senior citizens' centers in most communities now. Some of them are run by churches, some by community organizations, and some by private sources, volunteer or paid (they're called clubs). Depending on the support they have from community, municipal, and private resources, as well as from volunteers in the community or congregation, these centers may offer a variety of services to older people. A volunteer may come and wash a woman's hair, for example, or shave a man, if he lacks the strength to do it for himself. There may be foot clinics, cooking courses, mild exercise classes, and dances, too, depending upon the amount of ingenuity and enthusiasm of the people who run the centers. Volunteers can help old people shop or go to the doctor or deal with government letters and forms that are often confusing and frightening (bureaucracy always is). Some of them will help you with your income tax return—if you still make enough income to be taxable.

There is often a nutritionist on staff either at a senior citizens' center or at a local community health center in your area. The nutritionist can help you plan your meals to insure ease of preparation and maximum nutrition and supply you with booklets and pamphlets to help you in your shopping and menu planning. If you can't find such a person and such help, check out the information supplied by the federal government and other sources. There are tons of advice and helpful hints, usually yours for the asking, that may help you solve your nutritional and shopping problems.

Here's another suggestion, one so simple you'll laugh. Write letters. Don't laugh. If your hands aren't too sore, if you can spell, and even if you can't, pick up your ball-point and write. Write away for things. Get free samples. It'll make your mailbox interesting. Write your congressman; he/she has to answer—it's good for the image. Write complaints or kudos to manufacturers. They'll answer too, and probably send you more free samples. Find a pen pal. And, of course, if you have distant children and other relatives, be such a good correspondent that if you were playing tennis you'd beat them hollow, the ball is back in their court so fast. Sooner or later, they'll respond, even sons.

All these are things you can do to keep the world coming to you without stirring out of your room. If you have more than a room, and a little more energy, issue some invitations. By this time you know when the bad times are. Reach out to others then. Share a seasonal downer with them and turn it into a high spot. Beat the Anniversary Reaction. Phone a senior citizens' home, if you aren't in one yourself, and invite two or three of the more active women to join you in your kitchen to bake Christmas cookies, or Easter or Hanukkah bread, or whatever. If you can't afford the price of all the ingredients, ask them to chip in. They'll love the chance to putter in a real kitchen again and to have some home-baking to take back to share with their friends, and you have solved another day of the blahs. You can also do this with your grandchildren, should you be so lucky as to (a) have any (b) in the same city or town. But don't expect their mothers to be pleased with the kids' greasy clothes and full tummies when they return home. Grandmothers are notorious for being a bad influence—I think it skips a generation.

Go back to the piano you're sorry you neglected when your parents nagged you to go and practice; read all the books you never had time to get around to; learn a foreign language; take up painting, and think of Grandma Moses! Your work is over. Why not give yourself a treat? In doing so, you are doing yourself and the society you live in the biggest service of all. *You are asserting your right to be here.* In her book *The Second Sex* Simone de Beauvoir deals uncompromisingly with the problem of age for a woman. "When she has given up the struggle against the fatality of time," writes de Beauvoir, "another combat begins: *She must maintain a place on earth.*"

You have to keep on having goals in sight. You were not meant to languish in apathy. God grant you your health and your wits and enough money to keep food on your table and a roof over your head so you can keep on truckin'.

It's never too late, as the saying goes. You need not only spirit and wit and means; you need enough *anger* not to let anyone do you in, let you down, put you off, rub you out. In the old days this anger was, I believe, called backbone. It's backbone that is going to give you the strength to keep on doing your own thing. Heaven knows you have the freedom. This is one of the ironies of widowhood, all along the way, that you have been granted unique freedom.

"Strange that creatures without backbones have the hardest shells," wrote the poet Kahlil Gibran. *You* have backbone, so don't bother acquiring a shell. Stay soft. Stay open. Hang loose, as they say. Don't harden with resentment or self-pity. Don't tyrannize other people with your needs. Don't blackmail your children with your love. A free gift of love is infinitely more valuable. Wait for it. You have all the time in the world.

That's what I keep telling myself. I have all the time in the world, and I do. By the time I'm eighty-five, my marriage is going to seem like an interlude in my life, occupying, as it will have, less than one-quarter of it.

There are a lot of women like me; some 32 percent of the widowed are bereaved when they have at least half, if not more, of their adult lives to live. By the same token, 68 percent of widows are over the age of sixty-five, and, life expectancy statistics being what they are, they still have some living to do, too, alone.

The key word, of course, is *alone*. Children or no, young or not, you do everything alone and you face the terrible temptations of wallowing in self-pity or of enjoying sympathy, however and wherever it is offered.

"These temptations come," a widower wrote me, "because that special understanding, so generously given and so esteeming, has abruptly gone, and there remains a struggle not to shrink and become less of a person." You cannot afford to be less of a person. You have too much time to put in. By 1980 the life expectancy of the average female baby was 77.5 years. But the longer you survive, the longer you can expect to live. If you reach the age of 65 you now have an expectancy of 81.4 years. The average age of widowhood is fifty-six. So the years stretch on ahead, like a long tunnel of time, and what are you going to do with them? After the children have left, after you have retired from your work, and after other women friends have joined your ranks (Welcome to the Club), there remains your own cycle of days to put in before your time is up. Sooner or later, most of us will be aging lonely widows. You can't argue with statistics. The question is: do you have the means to cope with this last challenge life is throwing at you? By "means," I include everything financial, physical, mental, and spiritual. This is where the investments of a lifetime really begin to pay off. But if you haven't made them in the past, don't worry. You have a Creditor who will give you great support without collateral. And God is the one visitor who will always come when you call, no matter what time or day it is. You're just the person He was waiting to hear from.

You have proved your dogged endurance, your stamina, your innate sense of timing, and your skill at long distances. As you get older why not enjoy it? By this time you have earned a right to your knobs, your nonconformities. You don't have to diet anymore—at least not for appearance's sake, though you must guard your health. You can be outspoken and opinionated and eccentric—as long as you remain nice enough to retain your visiting privileges.

"Want to have some fun on your next birthday?" reads a contemporary card. "Paint racing stripes on your cane." I hope this has supplied the paint.

Sympathy, haircuts and assorted problems

What is the world to a man whose wife is a widow?

IRISH PROVERB

People have odd attitudes toward the bereaved, almost as odd as their attitudes toward death. They attend the funeral, and bury both halves of the couple—or seemingly so. The sight of a recent widow seems to be too much of a reminder of mortality, so they try to avoid her. When they do run into her, usually by accident and not by design, they are oversolicitous about her health. They tell her how fine she is looking.

She isn't. She looks like death warmed over. She hasn't started to eat or sleep with any regularity yet. How can she look like anything but what she is—a lost soul? I could tell when I really started looking better. People stopped telling me I was looking better.

"You're looking better?" they kept saying hopefully with a question. As if you'd been sick. And of course you were, sick to your soul.

You have suffered one of the most traumatic blows it is possible to suffer. You may be walking around upright, but your mind is still on crutches. Well, don't blame people. I've done the same thing myself, both before and since my husband's death. There is something awe-inspiring, silencing, and shattering about emotional pain that does leave one at a loss for words. Perhaps gestures are better. I've mentioned before my need for hugs. I'm sure other people feel the same way. Human physical comfort, no strings. I saw a cartoon once, no caption, which said it all. It was a vending machine; the sign on it read: "Hugs, 25¢." I wish I could have one installed.

It's not that people lack compassion. I do believe that most people think of themselves as kind and well-meaning. They're busy, they're shy, and they're tactless. So maybe if someone told them how to treat a widow, or anyone who has been recently bereaved, it would help us all. And maybe it would also help the bereaved, because they don't always know what they want and wish someone else would figure it out for them.

Listen. Just listen. More than anything, in the first few weeks of horror following a death, the widow needs someone to listen to her. She has to relive the death, relive the life she and her husband shared, begin to establish a new relationship with him and with the world she's still living in. She desperately needs to talk. Give her time. Let her talk.

Talk about him with her. Too many people clam up about the dead. It's not going to make her feel worse to talk about him; it's going to make her feel better. Recall funny things he said, nice things he did, good times you had together. My husband was a very witty man. Some of the nicest sympathy letters I received were ones in which the writer recalled some especially witty line he had said.

Conjure up for her the life she had. She has to confront it, look at it, and eventually start to withdraw. Help her to do so. He is still a living presence to her. She'll stop in time. Probably her own good sense will tell her when. One of the really horrible things I did was to talk about my husband on my first dates with other men. Like non-stop. That was hardly fair. It took me a while to realize what I was doing, and then I shut up. It's a test of others' tolerance and good will, I suppose, but it's a wonder they didn't hand me a memorial candle to light and leave.

Invite her over. But don't just say, "Drop in anytime," because she won't come. She's feeling hypersensitive and she may have already suffered a few rebuffs or indications that she's not as welcome as she was when she was part of a couple. One of the nicest things any couple did for me was to ask me to their place for a nightcap frequently after choir rehearsal. I used to dread going home at night after a meeting, because there was no one to tell about it and the children were in bed. It's something else you have to get used to.

Another couple used to ask me for a TGIF drink on Fridays, and that made me feel as if weekends weren't all bad.

So be specific in your invitations to a widow. Say when. And it wouldn't hurt to make it for dinner once in a while. That applies for months after the fact. If you're feeling guilty because you haven't done anything about poor Mary Smith, it's never too late. She's still alone. Ask her for dinner, preferably on a night when your husband is home. She won't eat him.

Hang in there. So many people, as I have indicated, drift away. Try for a few months, anyway, to give her some regular time. Maybe you could plan a weekly or monthly shopping excursion, something special, or a visit to an art gallery, or a swim, or a walk in the park—anything, just so it's planned and regular and forces her to think ahead a bit, plan for an event in the future, however simple.

Don't give her unsolicited advice. Don't tell her what to do. Don't make harsh judgments of what she has done. She's supersensitive anyway. If she wants your advice, she'll ask for it. I had one friend, within the week of my husband's death, criticize his insurance provisions for me and my family. What could I do about them then? In any case, they were what we had both agreed upon. We had always planned that I would work if he died early (never thinking that he would), and so we planned for a thin bottom line and spent our money on other things, like travel together. I am grateful for my memories.

Don't save up all the hard luck stories to tell her, expecting her to realize that she isn't the only one with problems. She knows that, but she's having enough trouble coping with her own right now. Telling her others doesn't make her feel any better.

I had one friend who, whenever we got together, at one point would nod her head wisely and say sententiously, "There are worse things than death." It was home-truth time, and she wanted me to know how lucky I was that I didn't have a living vegetable tied up to tubes in the hospital, or a human skeleton wasting away with pain in front of my eyes. I know, I know. We are given enough strength, I hope, to bear our own pain. I would not trade with others, nor they with me, in all likelihood. Sufficient unto the day.

Don't say, "You're lucky. You still have your children." It's true, they are blessings. But the widow doesn't feel very lucky and resents being reminded that she still owes a debt of gratitude. She'll come around to it.

Don't say, "He had a long, full life." Not full enough as far as she's concerned, and not nearly long enough. I had one widow whose husband died at sixty-six say to me that she felt it was too soon and unfair for him to die so young, forgetting that mine had died at forty-five. Tact takes a lot of practice and we all need it.

Do try to remember whom you're talking to. I ran into one woman in the supermarket shortly after my husband died who started telling me that her husband was away on a business trip and she said, "You know how much you get done when they're away and not underfoot." Yes.

"You're so free-wheeling," exclaimed a friend, commenting on the fact that I had driven myself in and out of Toronto (to a business appointment) in a day. "I wouldn't do that except under duress." Or because there's no alternative.

"You're getting so much thinner," exclaimed the same friend. "I envy you." Envy?

"There's someone you should meet," a friend told me. "She just moved in on the street next to you. You'll have a lot in common. Her husband's dead too." Common denominator?

"I guess the mistletoe isn't much use to you," said a friend at my first Christmas party A.D. "All the men here are married."

Don't say, "Cheer up—maybe next time you'll marry a rich husband." I know one widow to whom this was said at graveside. It was six months before someone said it to me. It's such a classic gaffe, I couldn't believe it was actually being said and I laughed out loud.

Don't ask, right after the interment, if she wants to sell the house. Someone asked my mother during my father's terminal illness. Even vultures have the tact to circle a while before they land.

Don't tell her all your troubles with your husband, with the implication that she's lucky she's well out of it. She'll sympathize with your daily concerns, but she doesn't want a glimpse of husband-wife relations, not for a while.

And don't, don't, tell her how importunate your husband is in the bedroom. I can remember being almost sick with pain when a couple of friends started discussing their husbands' sexual behavior ("He's at me all the time, never leaves me alone"). That's dirty pool.

And, men (we're back to sex again, I'm afraid), don't figure on giving her a treat. But an arm or a shoulder in a friendly hug is okay.

Try, if you can, to remember anniversaries, or at least one milestone in her year. If something aids you in remembering her husband's death date, then write her a note or phone her or send her a rose the following year. She hasn't forgotten what day it is. Or, if you were close, and enjoyed celebrating their wedding anniversary with them, remember it with her. Say something. It won't bring up any pain she might not have experienced. It comforts her that you also miss him and remember the good times.

Remember the good times and the good friends. If I have sounded harsh or critical of some of the treatment I've had, please understand that these were exceptions. As one widow said to me when she found out I was writing a book about widowhood, "Be sure to write about friends." Yes. Where would any of us be without them? I count among my richest blessings the friends who supported and cared for me, and continue to do so, in my loneliness and pain. They think of ways to help me that I could never think of myself. They also think of turning up at moments of need.

And sometimes it's surprising who turns up. The old saying "You find out who your friends are" is true. Old old friends, of course, remain friends, steadfast and true. But sometimes new friends, people you thought were friends, turn out to have been couple-friends, or convenience-friends, or reciprocal-friends, and when you are no longer part of a couple, when it is no longer convenient to know you, or when you are less able to reciprocate favors or invitations, these people fall away. On the other hand, you will find to your surprise that some of the people whom you thought of as very friendly acquaintances, but not close, become your staunchest supporters and most thoughtful allies. You never know.

One of the most delightful therapeutic things that was done for me happened after I moved to my new home in Toronto. I was invited, by two couples whom I knew well but not intimately, to join their Gourmet Dinner Club. It seems they had suffered several separations in their ranks, and they decided there was as much continuity in a single with a floating partner as there was in a couple with a precarious marriage. I had never recovered my interest in cooking since Bill died. Having to plan menus and suggest recipes to the group, and also, of course, to produce again, was marvelous therapy. It lured me back into the kitchen. Another rule: Help her to find an interest.

117

Remember that the times when married people are most occupied, widows are probably unoccupied, particularly in the early months. I can remember sitting quietly in my living room early one Saturday evening in June, some six weeks A.D., with soft tears streaming down my face. Someone came whom I didn't know that well, but whom I liked. And we talked. And became better friends.

I remembered the timing and did exactly the same thing for a fresh widow later that fall. And made another friend.

Another time, just before the Stratford Festival opening, which always gives me an Anniversary Reaction, another seemingly remote friend dropped in with some flowers from her garden. And we talked.

If you're too far away to risk a drop-in call, then phone. Say, "Just thought I'd call," and take it from there. You can never go wrong by taking a little thought. And it's never too late. One widow warned me that the second year is in many ways as bad or worse than the first, because people think you must be over it by now and withdraw some of their support. She's still alone.

If you're going to a meeting or a dinner or something that you know the widow will be going to as well, ask her if she wants a lift. Sometimes she gets stubborn (I did) and proud and won't ask for help. But she hopes like hell someone else will think of it. I went to my daughter's high school graduation exercises alone, because I would not ask to go with anyone, and no one thought of asking me to go with them. I guess that's how I learned to go alone to things. It's either that, or stay at home.

People are wonderful in times of stress. They rally around when there's a death or a serious illness. Then they are kindness itself and they know what to do. But they—we—all tend to forget the dailiness of loneliness and the unrelenting pressure of having to do everything yourself. An occasional thought on a day that isn't special will be greatly appreciated and makes the load seem lighter. Try not to forget her in the daily rush.

A lot of these rules apply to both widow and widower. There are some differences between them and it might help to consider them.

A widow is going to have trouble with maintenance and home repair. If you're a male friend and happen to be handy, ask her if there's anything that needs fixing, or take a look around for yourself. One neighbor of ours noticed that some tiles had dropped off our pool and, without being asked, got some caulking mixture and replaced them. Wow.

A widower, on the other hand, is having trouble coping with the meals. Even if he has very young children and has a housekeeper, you can bet the standards aren't as high as they used to be. Take over a fresh pie, warm from your oven, or a cake, or home-baked bread.

Tell a widower, as tactfully as you can, when his hair needs cutting. Chances are it was his wife who reminded him, and she's not around to do it.

Ask him and his family to dinner. This applies to anyone, doesn't it? Breaking bread together is a comforting thing to do. It seems to assert normality, to say, as nothing else does, that life does go on. We all have to eat.

A widower told me he could fix a kettle but he couldn't select his own ties. He can clean the house all right, but what's he going to do when a chair needs recovering, and he can't figure out what color it should be? He can cook a roast of beef but he can't plan a week's menus and therefore he has trouble with the shopping list.

A widow, on the other hand, has trouble with fuses, car maintenance, and hanging pictures.

Both widow and widower are disoriented, and for much longer than you realize. They go through the motions of normality; they go about what remains of their lives and their business and they seem to be making normal responses to the demands of daily life. But they are only half there. They are conducting a constant inner dialogue with someone who is absent. They are staunching a wound that has torn a gaping hole in their psyches. They are suffering withdrawal symptoms of the most severe kind.

So what can you do? Don't withdraw from them. Give them your support and sympathy. Say you're sorry, and prove it.

❋ 11
Plan ahead

> *A man called on me the other day with the idea of insuring my life. Now I detest life insurance agents; they always argue that I shall some day die, which is not so.*
>
> STEPHEN LEACOCK

All right, you've been through it. Now, if *you* died last night, would your executor/trix have all the information he/she needed to make life easier for your survivors? Do you, in fact, have an executor? Have you made out a will?

If you were going away on a trip and leaving children behind, you'd leave instructions for the babysitter, wouldn't you? Rather complete ones, in fact, with the doctor's phone number, and the numbers of the plumber, TV and washer repairmen, and possibly even some suggested menus, and a plan of action. Consider your death, then, merely as a bigger trip with this exception: no one can reach you where you're going. They can't ask you questions then, so answer them before you go.

Few people leave adequate information. Somehow they seem to feel that preparation is like an invitation. It isn't. It's a kindness you can perform for your children or whomever you leave behind. It's not only the financial arrangements that you've made that others have to know about; it's also the fiddley details that no one else knows but you. You might even go so far as to plan your own funeral. I had an aunt who did that. Wrote her own obituary, too.

First the business. Take several sheets of paper and begin your list. You do have a will, don't you? Have one drawn up if you don't, and keep it updated, if your finances or possessions change. One copy should be with your lawyer and one with you. On your list, write down where it is. List your policies: life, disability, group, fire, automobile, house, etc., and indicate where they may be found. List your bank accounts and say where your passbooks are. Write down anything and everything you have: bonds, stocks, certificates, Individual Retirement Accounts, Keogh Plan, deeds, mortgages, contracts, the names of any business partners, and all papers connected with business arrangements. And tell where they are. Plus your tax returns, financial statements, guarantees and warranties on your possessions (such as stove or car). Where are the car keys and the car ownership registration? Where is the safety deposit box located, if you have one, and where are the keys to it?

It is a very good idea to write down the purchase price of any stocks you own, and the date of purchase—or perhaps you have your purchase receipts on file (where?). List also the maturity dates of your bonds, if you don't keep them at home. And if you don't—that is, if they're in your deposit box—be sure to have a list at home of the contents. Note, too, the expiration dates of any certificates of deposit or U.S. government treasury notes you may have. Write down your future financial obligations and decisions, such as mortgage payments or stock options. Or tell what your rent is and when it's due. Are there a series of post-dated checks outstanding on that, or on an item you may be buying on time? Make a list of any other post-dated checks you may have written. What about bank loans? Mention tax payments as well. Include receipts that would be required to make up your final income tax return, as well as income statements, and don't forget information concerning capital gains or losses. Write down a list of any gifts made, trusts established, charitable gifts (or obligations).

Now list the locations of any stored valuables like jewelry, furs, stamp collections. You might like to talk over with your children the disposition of some of your possessions. Maybe one of them has always secretly loved a particular ornament or painting and would love to have it. Find out now, and reach an agreement about it, verbal or written. Written is better.

List your credit cards and their location, including the duplicates. And don't forget your birth certificate and your Social Security card—no one can do a thing without them. Tell where the bills are kept, and list any outstanding debts, including contractual obligations such as cable TV, snow removal contracts, decorating contracts, things on order. List your current and ongoing expenses. List your book club memberships and magazine subscriptions so that something can be done about them. And any club memberships.

Nothing is more baffling than a bunch of keys whose locks are unknown. As a matter of fact, keys paralyze me. I have keys that are meaningless to me now but that somehow I'm afraid to throw away. I have a key that I think belongs to a locker I used when I was at university. If I ever go back in a time machine it could be useful. When I travel I never lock my luggage, because I can't identify the keys to any of my bags. I'm not recommending that you harbor unidentified keys. The ideal thing would be to label them. If you're so organized you already have, you don't need to read a list like this.

Tell where your appointment book is and make sure someone will be aware of any appointments you have that have to be cancelled. My husband had just begun a series with a dentist which I had to cancel. Does anyone know similar information about you? You should also have a record of your children's appointments and lessons so that they may be continued (or postponed as the occasion dictates). Do any of your children have a refillable prescription? Where is it?

What about their eyes? Where is the correction prescription? Where do you buy their glasses? Where are their birth certificates, passports, school records, medical records? Do any of them have bank accounts or trust funds established for them? Have they had special bequests from grandparents or from your husband that they don't know about? Obviously these questions apply more to younger children, but older ones don't always know everything about themselves, their business and possessions. Are there any insurance policies on them? I take out school insurance on my children each year. If you do that, you'll have to say where those papers are.

If you have any obligations to other relatives, say so. I'm thinking of women who may contribute some support to an aged parent, or who are helping out a child on his own. In the case of the children, the support will likely continue, since they will be beneficiaries of any life insurance you may hold and will inherit your estate. But what about a parent? I am told that it is possible for a widow to buy a contract called a "joint and last survivor annuity," usually on a two-thirds, one-third, basis, that is, two-thirds of it riding on your life, and one-third of it riding on the life of the person you want to take care of. It can, however, be determined in any proportion you see fit, in terms of the amount of money you're talking about. This will enable you to continue payments to a parent or in-law in the event of your death. It's very cheap, because the odds are against your parent's outliving you, quite bluntly. This kind of protection can also be arranged for a handicapped sibling or child, but it's much more expensive, because the odds are different.

The youngest of my four children, Matthew, is learning disabled and epileptic. When my other three children were all in university, I took out term insurance on my life, naming Matthew as sole beneficiary. That way, I figured that if I died suddenly within the next four or five years, there would be enough money to set up care for Matthew without disrupting his brother's and sisters' lives. At the same time—let me assure you—I take very good care of my children's only parent.

Now start listing names, addresses, and telephone numbers. Start with your lawyer, life insurance agent, casualty agent, accountant, banker, broker, and any other financial advisers you may have. Include your and your children's doctors, dentist, pediatrician, orthodontist, speech therapist—all the people you can think of that you have dealings with. It's a good idea to include the names of teachers, Scout leaders, maybe even a few of your children's close friends. And why not include your maintenance people: plumber, washer repairman, cleaning lady, etc. Who else? Your children know who your friends are, or do they?

Tell them where your Christmas card list is, or your address book, or both. They'll need names and addresses to inform distant relatives (distant geographically, that is) and friends of your death. And a Christmas card list is a handy source of names for pallbearers, if that's the kind of funeral you want. Or you can pick your own pallbearers and write them down. Include a few alternates, in case some of them go before you do. And while you're at it, include an alternate executor/trix for the same reason. Did you know you can stipulate that your executor receive a fee for services rendered? If you've made a deal with someone to take the children, write that down too, though that's probably in your will.

If all this paper work doesn't appeal to you, you can probably find a booklet distributed by a life insurance company that will give you a handy checklist. Then all you have to do is fill in the blanks. The only record I had of the whereabouts of my husband's will, insurance policies, and so on, was in a little piece of paper I had pulled out of a *Better Homes and Gardens* magazine a few months before. Bill had scribbled in the answers to that very short list. If he hadn't, I would never have known, for example, that his will was in the vault in the box office at the Stratford Festival Theatre, nor am I sure when we would have found that very important document. No one was using the box office. It was off-season.

One more thing. What about the funeral? Funerals are primitive, but they are for the living, not the dead. It took me a while to figure that out. Other people really do need to pay some physical heed to the passing of one from their midst, some nodding of the head, dabbing of the eyes, some salute, some farewell. A funeral with its attendant ritual and ceremony gives the immediate family some opportunity to begin the work of confrontation and withdrawal and provides a social event by which relatives and friends gather 'round and offer some comfort for what it's worth. Sometimes it's worth a lot.

Funerals have been much maligned lately. The high cost of dying has been the subject of a great deal of criticism, and ridicule has been hurled at the pussy-footing euphemisms of funeral parlance: The Loved One is resting in the Slumber Room. Satin-quilted caskets and embalming and grave liners are all part of the euphemistic approach to death. They are also part of the emotional blackmail people tend to get caught up in at a time like death. A high-class (read: expensive) funeral always costs more than the Departed would have spent.

Funerals have changed very little in format in this century. They're still stuffy and mid-Victorian. When you think how weddings have changed, with the participants writing their own vows, choosing their own blessings, prayers and music, and even location, you realize how backward funerals are. Few people plan their own funerals. Maybe we'd have some better ones if they did. I heard of a memorial service held for a young priest which was a real celebration of his life. People stood up and remembered things about him; tapes were played of his best sermons; a dance company that he had used in his life for his services performed at his memorial tribute.

You could do that too, if you planned ahead. I wish I'd thought of some of these things before Bill died.

Since his death, I have discovered that not all the people I once knew are in graveyards. Before, the only one I knew about who wasn't was the Canadian poet Pauline Johnson—her ashes are buried in Stanley Park in British Columbia. But here are some other picturesque resting places I have learned since. One friend whose home is beside an artificial lake put her husband's ashes in a thicket of trees on the other side of the lake from the house, all in view of her picture window. The Canadian actor Leslie Yeo told me that his wife Hilary Vernon's ashes are under a tree in the lovely farmyard garden of actress Pat Galloway and her husband, Dr. Bernhard Frischke. The ashes of Reverend Russell D. Horsburgh are buried in the crawl space under the exact center of the sanctuary of Zion United Church in Hamilton, Ontario. There is a plaque on the wall attesting to this fact.

Now, why didn't I think of something like that?

As it was, I was very traditional. I was taken to pick a double plot in Stratford cemetery, and my husband lies on the stage-right side. I bought a large gray marble stone with his name and birth date and death date on it—$500 plus tax. I was reminded of the line ''nothing's certain but death and taxes.'' Very appropriate to tax tombstones. For a little more I could have had my name and birth date put on it—a very popular custom there—all filled out but the last piece of information. I declined, saying I might drown in the South Seas and my body never be recovered, and that would be a terrible waste of stone-cutting. I honestly don't like that empty space waiting for me. Every time one of my kids gets sick I think maybe they'll beat me to that space. That's morbid.

Even during the neuter time of my post-amputative recovery I wrote in my diary: ''If I ever marry again, whose wife will I be when I die and where will I be buried?'' And the real cruncher is that I'm a terrible gardener. Every time I go and look at the sad geraniums I put in each year and the struggling Japanese yews I planted I say to my husband: ''Well, you always knew what a terrible gardener I am.''

One widow I know found herself washed up on a more alien shore than mine. She and her four children left Ohio after her husband suddenly died. She knew she would never return. She bought a single plot, one small marker, took a picture of it, and moved back to Canada with her kids.

Bodies take up a lot of space in graveyards. Some big cities and small islands have resorted to stacking. But the green spaces cemeteries provide are like oases in the concrete jungles that many of our cities have become, one of the few places where people can find some peace and quiet, one of the few places, indeed, that people still pray, outside of a church. Emotions still hover around the plot, no matter how much you may tell yourself your loved one isn't there, that it's just his earthly remains that are deposited.

My own emotions were both raw and ambivalent, I can see now, both toward the cemetery and the tombstone. It has taken me some time to recover my perspective and to acknowledge the value and need of these taboo symbols of our society. They are associated with death in our minds and we prefer not to think of them.

But we forget the very real pleasure and education people get from wandering in cemeteries and reading old tombstones. We get a sense of history and sociology from them, some idea of the average lifespan of an earlier generation, some hint of the anguish parents suffered in the loss of children to diphtheria or polio, and of the pain men suffered losing their wives in childbirth. (Modern medicine and antisepsis have changed the stories that tombstones tell.) If we cease to put up tombstones, and tombstones not only with dates but with bits of poetry and wry comments and details about the life or death of the person thus commemorated, future generations will lose a portion of our history that they are entitled to have. It's only fair that our posterity should be able to walk in quiet green spaces and puzzle over our marble memoirs and wonder about us. I want them to.

There is a lot to be said for cremation. Unfortunately for me, it wasn't said before my husband died, but I have had personal experience with it since. I moved my mother from her home city to live with me when she was becoming unable to care for herself. At the age of 82, you don't leave home without pause. She discussed her death with me, whatever time it might come, and asked me to have her remains cremated and taken back to rest in the plot beside my father. Of course, I agreed, not knowing that the sad task would be undertaken only five months later.

You can talk and talk about something in the abstract, but reality is staggering. On the day my mother's ashes were to be picked up, I woke up paraphrasing a song:

> This is the day they give ashes away
> With half a pound of tea.

I walked over to my neighborhood crematorium (truly—there is one a few blocks from where I live) and was handed a small brown cardboard box, all that remained of my mother on this earth. Oh, what a precious, painful burden it was as I carried her under my heart. I don't know how I managed to cross streets, my eyes were so blinded by tears.

God works in such mysterious, glorious ways. I arrived home in time to pick up my mail and opened a taped recording of a musical I had written for my church. I put the tape on and heard my words, set to beautiful music and beautifully sung:

> Peace, peace,
> So the angels sing.
> Bow down before your heavenly king.

I felt peace dropping on my heart, so gentle and so healing, like the love we receive from God.

My son Matthew was still living with me then, and I had asked him to hurry home before I set out for the airport to take Nana back to Winnipeg. I showed him the box and explained to him again, as I reassured myself, that the ashes within were merely the earthly remains of his grandmother, that she didn't need her tired body anymore, that she was free of it now and moving on. We both put our hands on the box, and I prayed aloud for all of us. The doorbell rang, announcing the arrival of the cab to take me to the airport. I put the box in my shoulder bag, picked up my suitcase, and said good-bye to Matt.

"Good-bye, Mom," he said. "Good-bye, Nana."

If we're going to talk about cremation, why not talk about transplants and the whole medical science of spare parts? Whether the remains are going to be burned or buried, there is no earthly reason why you shouldn't donate any good usable pieces so that others may live. Quite a lot of a human being can be recycled now, about twenty-five different bits, as a matter of fact, including the kidneys, bones, joints, bone marrow, corneas, brains, hearts, lungs, livers, intestines (for research), pancreas, temporal bones (in the ear), pituitary glands, skin, and I even heard of one doctor who needed an entire spine! God knows, you won't be using them where you're going, and if you do, He'll look after it.

If you retain some sort of vague idea about the literal resurrection of the body, that's all right, too. You don't have to worry. If Judgment Day really is a literal one-time event (and I have this theory about its occurring all the time on a time-warp), with all the people who ever lived all brought together at the same time, the spare parts and ashes will certainly be reassembled as well. If God can handle the traffic problem, He can do anything, and He *can* do anything. Consider giving your parts to a good cause—another human being.

I wish I had discussed this with my husband, but I can do something about me, at least. I have discussed it with my children. If I die on a trip, then I am to be buried where I fall, because a one-way trip in a box is too expensive. If I die here, the usable parts of me can be salvaged. My province has a form on the back of the driver's license with space to indicate what parts one is willing to spare in case of an accident. Whatever is left of me can be cremated and taken back to that double plot and planted stage-left beside my husband.

Why don't you take time now and think about it? Think it through. There are donor cards and forms for bequeathal to medical schools available from your nearest memorial society. Write the national association for information:

Continental Association of Funeral and
Memorial Societies
1828 L St., N-W. Suite 1100
Washington, DC 20036

Even if you give your body to science or to other people, it won't all be used. The remains still have to be disposed of, so you can't dispense with the problem completely. You still have to decide how to deal with what's left, and you should allow for the emotions of your survivors. Perhaps they would like to plant a flower on you or water your grave with the odd tear. Talk it over with them. It might save you or them some money, too. The average funeral and burial costs exceed $2,571, as of 1982. You can cut a few corners by asking for the cheapest casket, skipping the grave liner, and requesting no embalming, but you may get an argument from the funeral director, especially on the last item. One funeral director told me why: "Most funeral homes are manned twenty-four hours a day [another reason for the costs]; this means someone lives there. You can't stick the body in the garage for three or four days! Embalming can or may be necessary even in cases of closed casket to protect the public coming into the funeral home and the funeral director from one of the unpleasant aspects of death."

But let me tell you that embalming is not required by state law unless the deceased died of a contagious disease or will be held longer than 24–72 hours (the time varies with the state) before it is disposed of.

Viewing the body, I am told, is very important. It begins the grief work for everyone. You have to see it to believe it.

Certainly that's true for the immediate family. I'm not so sure that it's necessary or even desirable for "outsiders" to see the body; it is, finally, a matter of personal preference. It was one thing I knew for sure what my husband's opinion was. He had sounded off only a short time before his death on how much he hated an open casket. So I closed his—*after* our private family ceremony.

There are four basic services provided by a funeral home: 1) move the body, 2) embalm the body, 3) supply a casket (a casket is not required for cremation), and 4) provide the facilities of the funeral home for viewing and/or the ceremony. The general services of the funeral director are included in the overall fee. You can get an itemized list of goods and services, and you can get prices over the phone so that you need not be trapped by emotion and inertia once you're in the funeral home.

If the high cost of dying worries you, why not investigate memorial societies? There are memorial societies in every state, including Alaska and Hawaii, and they have reciprocal arrangements with societies in Canada. The societies are non-profit, non-denominational, and, understandably, not too popular with funeral directors. A memorial society will help you to the simplest, most inexpensive form of burial or cremation you want. There are actually three types of memorial societies:

1) a contract society, with which you have a prearranged agreement for the type of funeral you want at a moderate cost
2) a co-operating society, which helps members make their own arrangements but without a prearranged contract
3) an advisory society, which simply advises its members. It has no preset agreements with funeral homes.

You could join a funeral society now and save your survivors a few more decisions. A family or individual membership will cost between five and twenty-five dollars, one time only.

· There is a Cremation Association of North America, too, with branches around the country. Membership costs between fifteen and twenty dollars and enables you to put your name and wishes on file. But most funeral homes offer cremation as well.

If that's what you want. Some people want pomp and panoply. I had an aunt, the one who wrote her own obituary, who demanded the most expensive casket available. She said she'd never had a Cadillac in her lifetime so she wanted a Cadillac of coffins when she died. She got it.

But my funeral director friend takes exception to my expression "pomp and panoply" and to my reference to a Cadillac of coffins. He reports to me the following statistics: "25 percent of the public want either a concrete vault or an airtight casket (Cadillac?); 94 percent said they would like a funeral service; 100 percent of widows said they would use a funeral home again; 96 percent of widows said there was an adequate selection of funeral types; 91 percent of the public attend a friend's funeral; 86 percent say they want their friends and relatives around at a time of loss; 72 percent say a religious service helps." In short, we the public are very traditional.

Perhaps I have done undertakers a grave injustice, if you'll pardon the pun. Certainly we need to do something to acknowledge the passing of someone from our midst, and we need help to do it. No one would argue with that. To leave life certainly requires a proper good-bye, and a proper good-bye gives everyone a chance to shake down and realize that a departure has taken place.

Then, too, the lead car behind the hearse is as close as you can get to an acknowledgment of your own mortality. Next time up, it's your turn. It's not all bad to face that fact.

And funerals and cemeteries also provide comfort in a tangible way. The survivors get to *do* something for the one who has died. We all know the soul has gone on, but we respect and handle with care the earthly temple of that dear soul—yes, even if we reduce it to ashes. I carried my mother's ashes back to be buried beside my father, and I carried that dear burden under my heart with love and pain.

Love doesn't die with the body. We need ways to express our love even after the body is no longer present. A lot of us in our human, finite way have difficulty comprehending God's infinite love for us. That's why we use art and music, texture and sound, and inspiring words and soaring prayers to help us fully realize that presence and encompassing love. So it's understandable if we want to do the same on a smaller scale to keep some feeling of the presence of our loved one with us. If you are traditionally inclined and want to go through the formal ceremonies of a funeral with all the trimmings, by all means do it. But be creative. Let your farewell be joyous and grateful. You have parted for a while. Today is not forever.

Most people think they're immortal, until it's proved otherwise. This seeming inability to envision one's own death, coupled with a general shrinking from the subject on the part of society at large, leaves most people completely unprepared for death, whether it's sudden or after a prolonged illness. As a matter of fact, in the case of a diagnosed terminal illness, the silence can often be worse. I know several widows and one widower who maintained, by some sort of mutual tacit agreement, complete silence about the impending death of their respective spouses. Neither party was willing to call a spade a spade, let alone acknowledge the imminent need to dig a grave with one.

Death is the only obscenity left in our society, the taboo that everyone still observes. I suppose it's fear of the unknown. But you and I know, don't we?

I'm not afraid of dying and death. It's living that's hard.

❋12
Help is on the way

> *God help those who do not help themselves.*
> ADDISON MIZNER

This is a do-it-yourself age we live in. Books and courses abound in self-help projects ranging from furniture upholstery to self-hypnosis. The magazines and newspapers are full of advice about anything that's troubling you, from dry skin to weekend guests, and they give short courses in everything from dog-training to balancing a budget. Entire bookstores are devoted to nothing but can-do books. There are information services provided by just about every business you can name, with pamphlets available on request, teaching the consumer how to use the product in question. Often the product is information itself.

So?

You might be the most competent person in the whole world, and you certainly know how to read directions, but you can't help feeling paralyzed when it's all laid on your shoulders—everything, all the maintenance, all the decisions, everything. And there are times when you just don't know where to turn, who to ask, how to find the answers you need.

What you need first is the sure and certain knowledge that you are going to survive. It said that in the newspaper, didn't it? "He is survived by his wife." Your back may be against the wall; you may be driven to tears, but you will not be driven to total collapse. And even if you are, well, there's help for that, too.

One of life's ironies is this survival. More than one widow has said to me, "Isn't it ironic that I had to lose my husband to find myself?" People have said that to me, commenting on my second trajectory career as a writer, wondering whether I capitalized unfairly on my husband's death. Bill always used to say if you get a lemon, make lemonade. If I had my druthers, I'd ruther he were alive and well and still with me. But he's not.

I can't begin to give you all the information you need, but I can give you the reassurance. You will find a way out of this maze of pain and bewilderment. Everyone has a different weak spot, but there are ways of compensating for it. I get paralyzed by things I have to do that I call "fiddleys—" time-consuming, annoying, unproductive, fiddley details that have to be looked after. I have a friend who feels the same way I do. Know what she did? She hired a college student on a part-time basis, so much an hour, to do her fiddleys for her. She spends less on that than she would spend on a cleaning lady, and she doesn't mind cleaning her own house. Her part-time organizer has done things like this for her: renewed her passport, taken inventory of her possessions for insurance evaluation, ordered her children's winter underwear, returned things that aren't suitable. None of these things is difficult, but they're fiddley. My friend is much more relaxed now.

Every once in a while when I am in danger of going down in a sea of paper, I hire a student like that to come and make sense of my files for me. Thirty hours of sorting and filing can make a new woman of me!

The most fiddley thing I have to do each year is work on my income tax. It really is fiddley because I am a free-lance writer and my income comes from a lot of different sources. I also have fiddley expenses that must be kept track of, like parking and postage, paper, and books, and typewriter ribbon (and now—floppy disks!), and all stuff like that. I bought a cheap calculator, at my son's suggestion, to help me put my receipts in order before I go to a tax accountant to help me. Some widows I know say they feel a real thrill of accomplishment when they work out their own income tax forms. I'd go to jail before I achieved that thrill. I choose to use the help available. One tax deduction I might not discover pays for the accountant's services, and his services are deductible, too.

If you have other financial problems, there are experts around to talk to you, besides books and brochures to read, and courses to take. Your banker doesn't charge; maybe he's the one to start with. Talk to a friend's husband who you think knows what he's doing (but don't ask for a private consultation). If you do have to go to a lawyer or a professional consultant, just remember that his/her rates per hour are high, so do your homework as I do for my accountant. Prepare your material, your questions, and your information so that you will use as little as possible of that expensive professional time in the briefing before you ask your questions. You will then be paying for expertise and not for paperwork.

If you have a job problem, you're not alone—but that's no help. At a certain level of education and skill, there are head-hunter organizations that will help you find a job in your field, for a fee. In the past few years there have been waiting lists for the lower-paid, unskilled jobs, which are not too rewarding when you get them. You may need more than advice; you may need training so as to bring your skills up to a higher paying level. There are resources in each community that you can turn to for guidance. Don't forget the biggest resource you have is yourself, your own determination and spirit.

If you already have a job and are having trouble, go to the personnel officer in the company, or if it's too personal a problem, talk it over with a trusted friend. I have heard of a few large companies that have recognized the stress of bereavement and that conduct workshops to help their employees over this bad time. You might even suggest it in your firm.

What you have to have is a positive attitude. *Of course,* this problem can be solved. *Of course,* you're going to solve it. You solved the last one, didn't you? Each time you solve a problem successfully, it gives you much more confidendce for the next one. That's what I keep telling myself, but someone keeps thinking up new problems!

If you really can't cope, if the world is too much with you, and you feel too discouraged and bogged down to carry on, you could go to your doctor. But don't accept a course of tranquillizers without attempting a long-term solution to your problem. Treat the cause, not the symptom. Go to your minister or rabbi, or make an appointment with a counselor, or get your doctor to refer you to a psychiatrist if things are really bad. It wouldn't hurt to pray.

Some organizations and services that a widow may find helpful are self-explanatory and fairly easy to find, such as the Big Brothers organization, or the local chapter of Parents Without Partners, for those women with children still at home. Other groups defy discovery. Just keep asking questions.

Self-help groups are most effective. A widow-to-widow program was first developed by the Harvard Medical School, modelled after the Widows' Consultation Centre in New York. It has been discovered that another widow is the surest, most effective aid a widow can have. The old line "you have to have been there to know what it's like," is so true it hurts. No one but another widow can reassure you that you are not going insane, and that you will survive.

Churches, Ys, and community service organizations as well as enterprising individuals across the country are beginning to recognize the very real needs of the bereaved and to take the responsibility for meeting it. Grief and loneliness are legacies of bereavement which must be faced and treated. Nothing is quite so difficult when there is sympathy, practical help, a chance to communicate one's feelings, and guidance along the way.

And so there is a growing movement of self-help programs for widows. The National Association for Widowed People was founded quite recently and has grown rapidly in response to the need, with chapters springing up across the country. According to its information brochure, it is both a social organization and a community service for men and women of all ages who have lost a spouse. There are trained volunteers who staff a telephone line to help recently bereaved persons. There is, as well, a service called IN TOUCH, enabling widowed people to get acquainted with each other, a travel club, and a job service that helps those who need employment to assess their skills and to find a job.

For further information write the national headquarters of NAWP, P.O. Box 3564, Springfield, Illinois, 62708. If there isn't a chapter in your area, perhaps you are the one meant to get one going.

There is also the Widowed Persons' Service, run by the National Retired Teachers' Association. For more information, write this organization at 1909 K Street, N-W., Washington, D.C., 20049.

Don't be afraid to ask for help. Yelp and holler a little. *Someone* will hear.

Six months after Bill died, I went to a seminar on healing, seeking some solace for my emotional and spiritual wounds. During that weekend, one of the assignments was to "walk to Emmaus." That was the walk on which two men discussing the remarkable events they had heard about over Passover weekend in Jerusalem, involving the—would you believe it?—*resurrection???* of a body? They were joined by a man who walked with them all the way to Emmaus.

We were told to take that walk alone, and see who joined

us. Well, two people joined me: my husband and that Other Guy.

That was the beginning. I bought a little book that weekend that became my constant bedside companion for a year. As fast as I finished it, I began again at the beginning. *Letters from the Scattered Brotherhood* taught me how to meditate.

That's how I stumbled on Christian meditation. Transcendental meditation was very popular at the time, but there is a long tradition of Christian meditation in the Western world, and I found it suited me very well. Instead of meaningless sounds I used lines from the Bible as my mantras. There are wonderful, reassuring texts that offer comfort as well as concentration. In time I found the one that was most effective for me.

"God is love" is a simple one. Some people, I am told, just say "peace" over and over again. Mine is quite long but it is so powerful that it soothes and calms me in the saying of it.

Be still, and know that I am God.

It is a direct command and centres me as nothing else can. Alone as I am— as any of us is—in this dark tunnel of time leading to reunion with our loved ones, that reassurance gives me the light at the end of the tunnel. Be still. Be still. Everything is going to be all right.

Bibliography

Aries, Phillipe. *The Hour of Our Death*. New York: Knopf, 1981.

Bel Geddes, Joan. *How to Parent Alone*. New York: The Seabury Press, 1974.

Bolles, Richard N. *What Color Is Your Parachute? A Practical Manual for Job-Hunters and Career-Changers*. Berkeley, CA: Ten Speed Press, Box 4310, 94704. Edited annually.

Caine, Lynn. *Widow*. New York: William Morrow & Company, 1974.

Chesler, Phyllis, and Emily Jane Goodman. *Women, Money and Power*. New York: Bantam Books, 1976.

De Beauvoir, Simone. *The Second Sex*. New York: Bantam Books, 1968.

Edwards, Marie, and Eleanor Hoover. *The Challenge of Being Single*. Hawthorn Books, 1975.

Gladstone, Bernard. *The New York Times Guide to Home Repair Without a Man*. New York: Quadrangle/New York Times Company, 1974.

Glick, Ira O., Robert S. Weiss, and C. Murray Parker. *The First Year of Bereavement*. New York: John Wiley & Sons, 1974.

Grollman, Earl A., ed. *Explaining Death to Children*. Boston: Beacon Press, 1967.

Harmer, Ruth Mulvey. *The High Cost of Dying*. Collier Books, 1963.

Hite, Shere. *The Hite Report*. New York: Dell Publishing, 1976.

Jackson, Edgar N. *Telling a Child About Death*. New York: Channel Press, 1965.

Keleman, Stanley. *Living Your Dying*. New York: Random House, 1974.

Kubler-Ross, Elisabeth. *Death: The Final Stage of Growth*. New Jersey: Prentice-Hall, Inc., 1975.
On Death and Dying. New York: Macmillan, 1969.

Kushner, Harold S. *When Bad Things Happen to Good People*. New York: Schocken Books, 1981.

Lewis, C. S. *A Grief Observed*. London: Faber & Faber, 1961.

Lifton, Robert Jay, and Eric Olson. *Living and Dying*. New York: Bantam Books, 1974.

Miller, Jean Baker. *Toward a New Psychology of Women*. Boston: Beacon Press, 1977.

Mitford, Jessica. *The American Way of Death*. New York: Fawcett Crest. 1963, with 1979 update.

Nelson, Paula. *The Joy of Money*. New York: Stein and Day, 1975.

Peterson, James, and Barbara Payne. *Love in the Later Years*. New York: Associate Press, 1975.
Porat, Dr. Frieda, with Karen Meyers. *Changing Your Life Style*. New York: Bantam Books, 1973.

Porter, Sylvia. *Sylvia Porter's New Money Book for the 80's*. New York: Doubleday, 1979.

Pincus, Lily. *Death and the Family: The Importance of Mourning*. New York: Vintage/Random House, 1974.

Selye, Hans. *The Stress of Life*. New York, Toronto, London: McGraw-Hill, 1956.

Starr & Weiner. *Sex and Sexuality in the Mature Years*. New York: Stein and Day, 1981.

Taves, Isabella. *The Widows' Guide*. New York: Schocken Books, 1981.

———*Women Alone*. New York: Funk & Wagnalls, 1968.

Vogel, Linda Jane. *Helping a Child Understand Death*. Philadelphia: Fortress Press, 1975.

You. *The Nothing Book*. Warner Books, NOW.

Booklets and Pamphlets

American Association of Retired Persons
Widowed Persons Service
1909 K Street, N.W.
Washington, D.C. 20049

> *On Being Alone*, James A. Peterson.
> AARP, Widowed Persons Service
> Box 199, Long Beach, CA
>
> *Widowed Person Service Organization Manual*
> (available only to groups organizing
> as AARP Widowed Persons service
> programs) Washington address (see
> above)

American Council of Life Insurance
Health Insurance Association of America
1850 K Street, N.W.
Washington, D.C. 20006

> *Let's Talk About Money*
> *New Group Disability Insurance*

New Group Health Insurance
The Money Manager: Step-by-Step to
Money Management
What You Should Know About
Disability Insurance
What You Should Know About Health Insurance
What You Should Know About IRAs

Continental Association of Funeral and
Memorial Societies, Inc.
1828 L Street, N.W., Suite 1100
Washington, D.C. 20036

Directory, up-to-date listing of memorial
societies in US and Canada.
Information on Anatomical Gifts
Facts About Cremation
Forms for Bequeathal to Medical School
(3 for $1.50)

Household Finance Corporation.
Money Management
Booklet Library.
Set of twelve booklets.
Prudential Plaza
Chicago, Illinois 60601

Index

ABOUT THE AUTHOR

Betty Jane Wylie, a journalist and playwright, is active in many associations that provide help and advice for widows and is in much demand as a public speaker. Born in Winnipeg, Canada, she has had plays produced in Canada, the United States, Bermuda, Great Britain, and New Zealand. In addition to the publication of twelve plays, twelve non-fiction books have been published, ranging in subject matter from biography to financial planning to cooking. *Beginnings*, which was written in response to an unprecedented readers' reaction to an article on widowhood for the Canadian magazine *Maclean's*, is a Canadian bestseller, published as well in Great Britain and Australia.

Faith and Fulfillment...

BALLANTINE/EPIPHANY BOOKS